# WERE YOU THERE?

# WERE YOU THERE?

## FINDING OURSELVES AT THE FOOT OF THE CROSS

*Erik Kolbell*

WESTMINSTER
JOHN KNOX PRESS
LOUISVILLE · KENTUCKY

Scripture quotations from the Revised Standard Version of the Bible are copyright © 1946, 1952, 1971, and 1973 by the Division of Christian Education of the National Council of the Churches of Christ in the U.S.A. and are used by permission.

Lyrics from "Brokedown Palace" by Robert Hunter, copyright Ice Nine Publishing Company. Used with permission.

Lyrics from "The Boy in the Bubble" by Paul Simon are Copyright © 1986 Paul Simon. Used by permission of the publisher: Paul Simon Music.

*Book design by Sharon Adams*
*Cover design by Pam Poll Graphic Design*

*First edition*
Published by Westminster John Knox Press
Louisville, Kentucky

This book is printed on acid-free paper that meets the American National Standards Institute Z39.48 standard. ∞

PRINTED IN THE UNITED STATES OF AMERICA

05 06 07 08 09 10 11 12 13 14 — 10 9 8 7 6 5 4 3 2 1

**Library of Congress Cataloging-in-Publication Data**

Kolbell, Erik.
     Were you there? : finding ourselves at the foot of the cross / Erik
Kolbell.— 1st ed.
          p. cm.
     Includes bibliographical references.
     ISBN 0-664-22778-3
     1. Jesus Christ—Biography—Passion Week.     2. Jesus Christ—
Friends and associates.     I. Title.

BT414.K63 2005
242'.35—dc22
                                                           2004057194

To William Sloane Coffin Jr.
*a giant of a man*

# Contents

# Foreword

*I*nteresting that every first-rate book we read is of two minds—the mind of the book itself, the story it tells, and the mind of the author, who unconsciously breathes his character into the narrative. It is this mind in the shadows that gives us something we want to hold on to, long after we have forgotten the story's details. I could not tell you half the things that happen in Conrad's novels, for instance, though Conrad is my favorite novelist. But I could talk a blue streak on what it feels like to be in the hands of one who could see into the heart of everything, darkness no more clearly than light.

So one takes up *Were You There?* Erik Kolbell's learned and generous study of the Passion of Jesus, and knows within a few pages that one is reading both the tale the author tells and that of the author himself. "The Passion," he writes, "is the story of one person with the echoes of many, and while I stand in awe of the one who laid down his life for me, I stand in sympathy with those around him, because in their stories I so readily see my own." Only a certain kind of man could write a sentence like that, because those around Jesus at the time of the crucifixion included cowards and traitors as well as the gentle and the valorous. That Kolbell sees the story whole suggests that he sees life whole, and thus the book he offers becomes not only admirable but also trustworthy.

This said, *Were You There?* is not a book without a spine. Kolbell never dilutes his morality in the interests of his humanity. His moral mind applies itself to ancient Jerusalem no more than to modern America, where these days the right to dissent is also threatened (should one say crucial?). To find oneself "at the foot of the cross," as Kolbell's subtitle suggests, is to acknowledge individual responsibility as well as sorrow. If Jesus died that others might live, then the quality of the lives that remain demands sacrifice and virtue, in homage to the one that was forfeited.

It is a very good thing that this book arrives so soon after Mel Gibson's divisive film on the subject, *The Passion of the Christ,* since the inclusiveness of Kolbell's humanity delivers a quite different and more persuasive message. In an earlier book, *What Jesus Meant,* Kolbell described Jesus as a rabbi who taught as a rabbi—a thought that in itself was healing to Christians and Jews. But the overarching truth here is that God's love allows for all the varieties of the human animal, and for all the sins and skepticism of which we are capable.

Mary comforts, Judas betrays, Thomas doubts, Peter swears and then renounces, Cleopas ignores, Joseph seeks, Simon helps, Caiaphas abuses power, as does Pilate, as does Herod. All those involved in the life and death of Jesus had choices, which is what Kolbell is getting at. The God who provides choice for his creations must know that some will fail, even to the point of the destruction of the earth, so he too has had to make a preemptive choice to love his creatures no matter what they choose. Love is not without judgment, but at the same time it is greater than judgment.

The last days of Jesus contain a story of monumental significance, not only because they redefine the concept of divinity, but also because they deal with human nature as it is tested most severely. The weak, careless, scared, cruel, brave, gentle, inspired people who were near Jesus at the end are around today, speaking different languages, wearing different hats, yet the same population. By dying, Jesus seemed to teach those around him not that death was unimportant, but rather that life was precious, and that what one does with it is of great moment and urgency. "Were You There?" is another way of asking, "Are you here?" That is the author's question to the reader.

—Roger Rosenblatt

# Preface and Acknowledgments

*T*he tale of the last days of Jesus of Nazareth is familiar to people from all religious backgrounds and people of no religion at all. Its themes of guilt and forgiveness, compassion and injustice, cowardice and valor, loyalty and betrayal, and the awesome power of life to prevail over death, are as old as civilization itself and as applicable today as they were when they were first told.

What makes them applicable, I think, is the fact that we cannot live our lives apart from these themes, for even if we do not consider ourselves answerable to God or gods, we are answerable to each other and to our own consciences. Even the most personal decisions we make affect others, directly or by inference, and if there is one element that threads itself throughout the Passion, it is accountability. All of the people—from the high and mighty to the weak and lowly—play a part in this great story, and the story itself would have been very different had any one of them not played those parts the way they did. This book is a modest effort to shine a little light on those people, to tell *their* stories, and to see how inextricably bound those stories are to the unfolding of history those many years ago.

I write this book because all of us are accountable for what we do or fail to do. It is what makes us human. All of us are capable of gestures of unconscionable turpitude and acts of unspeakable beauty. It is what makes us people of free will. And perhaps, in the end, we come to learn through our own stories that though death is strong, life is stronger. It is what makes us people of hope.

While I take responsibility for every word and idea in this book, I would be terribly remiss if I did not acknowledge four people without whom it never would have gotten written. In no particular order:

A deep thanks to my agent, Claudia Cross, for believing in the concept and encouraging me to believe in it too.

I am grateful beyond words to my editor, Stephanie Egnotovich, who wielded her pen as a surgeon would a scalpel, and who saw what I missed, challenged my assumptions (and did so firmly but gently), and always managed to tighten what was too loose and loosen what was too tight.

I have always been indebted to my wife, Ann, for more than the creation of this book. She has been generous with her wisdom and tireless in her support, and in the case of this project has allowed me a much-needed sabbatical from all chores domestic as I have pushed to meet my deadlines.

And I am so very thankful for our daughter, Kate, who leads by example. She is the most courageous person I have ever known.

# Introduction

*And the Word became flesh and dwelt among us, full of grace and truth.*

—John 1:14

*N*othing in human history has incited the passions quite like the Passion. The accounts of the last days in the life of Jesus have stimulated the thoughts of the five-year-old Sunday schooler, the jaded cynic, and the most profound philosophers since the Renaissance. The vernacular of the Passion has found expression in the arts as well as in psychology, mythology, literature, and, alas, often tragically, world politics. It is a story that has underscored Jesus' humanity and affirmed his divinity, inspired hope in some and fear in others, provided both the basis for a theology of peace and a pretense for the provocation of war. Once one has read the story, it is difficult to remain unmoved by it.

Many people read the Passion the way they might read ink blots in a Rorschach test: seeing what they are predisposed to see and thereby sanctifying their prejudices. In doing this, they may in their own minds, for instance, advance the myth of Christian supremacy, secure their belief in a celestial afterlife, concretize their faith in the power of redemption, or codify their sentiments of anti-Semitism.

Others try to do quite the opposite; they make every effort to approach the Passion the way the medieval mystics did, as a revelation from God to which they must bring no preconceptions. Instead of trying to interpret the text, they let the text interpret

them, making of their minds a kind of tabula rasa on which God
inscribes the story in such a way that, as literally the crux of the
faith, it profoundly changes who they are.

A third way of reading is to listen to where this extraordinary
story intersects with our own. This approach acknowledges the
subjectivity of the first and the objectivity of the second. The Passion is a story of God at work in history, and it is our bearing witness to that history, by experiencing and expressing it as the
Gospel writers did—as a story *"according to . . ."* None of the
evangelists—from Mark's austere description of the death of Judas
to John's supernal vision of "angels in white, sitting where the
body of Jesus had lain"—pretends to have recorded verbatim what
was said to have happened. But neither did they extemporize on it
so as to make of the events a fiction bent to fit their needs. What
each writer *did* do was give to us an honest reporting of real events
as seen through the lens of his own individual faith.

This means, in part, that they did not intend that the credibility
of the story rise or fall on how closely their account resembles
what transpired, and in what order, over the course of those few
days. Rather, they meant to convey the intense drama, pathos,
treachery, and love that were woven together in this unique
moment in time, to show how God's work was not imposed on that
time but rather came forth from within its confines. The Passion
story is not simply God made known to people; it is God walking
and working among those people.

And more to the point, the Passion is God's will being enacted
through their lives, each of which is not peripheral but central, not
accidental but intentional, not incidental but indispensable, to the
tale's unfolding. So Caiaphas would not have ordered the arrest of
Jesus to occur so quietly, had Jesus not been met with palms and
hosannas when he first entered Jerusalem. Likewise, Jesus would
not have been seized at Gethsemane, had Judas not betrayed him
or had the other disciples standing guard not fallen asleep. Even
the discovery of the resurrection would not have transpired the
way it did, had Joseph not asked to bury the body or had the
women not come to anoint it. In those lives, I believe, the Passion
can become so much more meaningful to us, because in these lives

we can find our own, and in so doing, we intimately intertwine our unique story with the one that came into view in the hills of Palestine so many years ago.

From the doubts of Thomas to the devotion of Salome (who anointed Jesus' body after the crucifixion), each person in the Passion story represents one point in the great range of human responses that is also available to us. When in our own lives we are called upon to make decisions that will have an effect—whether profound or sublime—on some part of our world, we can find ourselves reflected in these characters. The effect may be felt in a vote we cast or a job we take, an act of civil disobedience we do or do not engage in, or a decision to support an unpopular cause that is dear to our hearts. In Peter's denial we may see our own cowardice, and in Pilate's handwashing we may see our own hesitancy to accept the consequences of our actions. Likewise, though, in the repentant thief we hear echoes of our own humility and in Mary's courage we recognize that we too are capable of great strength.

> "Destiny is something not to be desired and not to be avoided . . . a mystery not contrary to reason, for it implies that the world, and the course of human history, have meaning."[1]
>
> —Dag Hammarskjöld

In suggesting that we can find ourselves in the lives of these people I am not arguing that the Passion be read one particular way over another. In fact, part of the beauty of the story is its fluidity. To some it is an intensely theological work that sketches out in narrative form the parameters of the Christian faith, while for others it is the fulfillment of Old Testament prophecy. Some of us try to stake our claim to its historical accuracy and others to its power as allegory. Any number of roads lead to the same destination, but once we arrive there, I believe we deepen our understanding of the story if we find our own lives paralleled in the lives of those who were there. The Passion does not, I believe, tell the tale of a kind of cosmic inevitability in which the everyday people are mere props, backlights on the great stage of Golgotha. It is instead the recounting of a series of human events, enacted by a broad cast of human beings, each very much embedded in the time and place in which they lived, and each subject to the sometimes discordant pull between their inherent personality and the influences that that time and place had on them. In the words of the historian Donald Creighton, "History is the record of an encounter between characters and circumstances."[2]

## There and Then

The Jerusalem that Jesus entered to meet his fate, the place where most of these people lived and worked, was a cosmopolitan oasis in a backwater land. There was a heavy dose of cultural and religious intermingling, as Jews lived side by side with Syrians, Greeks, Romans, and others, though the synagogue remained the focal point of the Jewish community and efforts were made to maintain the "purity" of Judaism by looking dimly on the religious practices of other cultures.

Governance over the region was a mixture of Roman and local rule. The Romans allowed the Jews their own king (Herod) and their own "parliament" (the Sanhedrin, overseen by the high priest, Caiaphas) but held ultimate authority in the person of a procurator (Pilate), who could override the decisions of the Jewish government if he so chose. This made for some obvious points of friction, because when occasions called for the Jews to resist Roman edicts, the Sanhedrin was unable to act, and Herod—spineless before Roman authority—was unwilling. So while Rome's despotism could at times be benign, it was despotism nonetheless. The Jews, a people with a once proud heritage as an empire in their own right, were now a kept people, and they knew the difference between being the ruler and the ruled.

And as with any occupied people, theirs was a society plagued by the kind of unhappiness that metastasizes into unrest. There were some who wanted open revolt and others who believed the only path to liberation was through prayer, study, and supplication before God. Others found their living conditions to be proof positive of the irrelevance of their religious tradition, drifted far from their native faith, and, in some cases, adopted the religious practices of their occupiers. There were some who believed a messiah would soon be sent by God to relieve them of their suffering, and others still who believed that anyone who made that claim would only be inviting more unhappiness, more uncertainty, and more unrest. It was, to say the least, a fractious time, made no less so by the fact that this was a land with a great disparity between the rich and the poor, where the king allowed forbidden idols to be placed in the temple, where the Roman government exacted heavy taxes, and where a large portion of the population was too disabled to support themselves.

In this environment we might expect to find the likes of a high priest who was more enamored with a firm power base than with a theologically invigorating discourse about the nature of salvation. Here also we would find one centurion whose devotion to his emperor was unquestioned and another for whom it was greatly disturbed by doubt. It was the kind of place that, when thrown into the turmoil it faced when Jesus entered, would be rife with intrigue, danger, betrayal, cowardice, valor, courage, kindness, and generosity, all in far greater measure than we are used to in our own lives.

## Finding Ourselves at the Foot of the Cross

The Passion is the story of one person with the echoes of many, and while I stand in awe of the one who laid down his life for me, I stand in sympathy with those around him, because in their stories I so readily see my own. The very best and the very worst of who we are come to play a constitutive role in Jesus' destiny, reinforcing the notion that the divine intention does not work itself out in a vacuum; God's work is truly our own.

And while we are not called regularly to face crises of such momentous proportion, there is no work we do that, if done in God's name, is inconsequential. As Gandhi once said in contemplating those in India with little or nothing to eat, "We can live our lives such that with every single thing we do we may ask ourselves

'How is this helping the poor of the world?' "[3] What he is saying, it seems to me, is that in all of the decisions we make, whether they appear to be momentous or mundane, we are always somehow either reflecting God's will or resisting it. When we refuse to trust what we know in our heart is right, there is a little bit of the doubting Thomas in us, and when we stay up long hours with an injured child and can do no more than keep company with her, we are a vague reflection of Mary, who could not take away her son's pain but also would not abandon him to it. We are people of faith not only sometimes, but everywhere and at all times. But whether we act as people of faith is another matter altogether. As the late statesman Dean Acheson once wrote, "The manner in which one endures what must be endured is more important than the thing that must be endured."[4]

So as we read these stories of scoundrels and saints and consider how they endured the Passion, we will discover intimations of our own lives, our own stories, and our own manner of shouldering the great burdens that our faith asks us to make.

Finally, I must mention that this book is by necessity highly speculative and that I take some license with the stories of these people. Imagine taking a bowl of fruit, placing it in a room with three chairs and three artist's easels, and putting Jasper Johns in one chair, Jenny Holzer in another, and my ten-year-old neighbor in the third. You ask them to draw what they see, as they see it. What you'd get is not a photographic replication of the fruit, or even a reproduction as *you* might see it, but impressions, as seen through the eyes of the beholders. The gospel "according to": none more valid than the next, and each in its own right an interchange between an immutable reality and the extremely dexterous imagination of the artist.

What I offer here is, unapologetically, my impression, my sense of how it may have been for these people of the cross. What they *might* have been thinking. What *might* have motivated them. How they *might* have behaved in situations not recorded in the Gospel narratives. It is their story meeting mine, not authoritatively but interpretively. I don't pretend to offer the unvarnished truth; I can only paint what I see.

And as to the order in which I present the chapters, it is chrono-logical. While I move freely among the Gospels for these stories, I present them in the order in which they were to have occurred.

I hope that as you work your way through this little book you will find that the characters in these pages are not strangers to you, but people with whom you share common experiences. I also hope you see in them people such as yourself, who knew, as we do, that living out our faith in a world so often hostile to it is both enor-mously difficult and eminently worthwhile.

# She Anointed His Feet

*To give and give, and give again, what God hath given thee; to spend thyself nor count the cost; to serve right gloriously.*

—*"Awake, Awake to Love and Work,"*
Geoffrey Studdert-Kennedy[1]

*And while he was at Bethany in the house of Simon the leper, as he sat at table, a woman came with an alabaster jar of ointment of pure nard, very costly, and she broke the jar and poured it over his head. But there were some who said to themselves indignantly, "Why was the ointment thus wasted? For this ointment might have been sold for more than three hundred denarii, and given to the poor." And they reproached her. But Jesus said, "Let her alone; why do you trouble her? She has done a beautiful thing to me."*

—Mark 14:3–6

*T*o love is good," wrote the poet Rilke, "love being difficult. . . . It is the work, for which all other work is but preparation."[2] And what is the Passion but a love story? Not the sentimentalized affection or self-pleasing eroticism shared by young lovers, but demanding love, love of the highest striving, love that does not count the cost. It is the extravagance of the alabaster flask broken and poured out for him, just as he would soon be broken and poured out for her.

To know "the work" of love is to know what it means to pour

yourself out for another. From birth to death it is the work of presence, of being unconditionally present to another's needs. And so it is pacing the floor with the six-week-old baby at two in the morning until her fever breaks, not for a moment thinking there is anywhere in the world you would rather be. It is traveling a long distance through the rain to pay a visit to a man who is recently widowed, who cannot seem to shake his depression, and whose friends have stopped coming by because "it's just too uncomfortable." In my practice as a psychotherapist I've seen the work of couples looking deep into their souls to find the love that has been lost to lassitude bred of familiarity, and I respect the nobility of their labors.

And when I think more deeply about what epitomizes the work

> I was doing premarriage counseling with a young couple who were quite certain they were soul mates. "I feel like I know *everything* there is to know about Josh," the bride-to-be told me. "I know his values, and his passions, and his pleasures . . ." I then stopped her and posed this question: "But do you know whether he squeezes the toothpaste tube from the middle or from the bottom?"
>
> She looked at me quizzically, confessed that she didn't, and then asked, "But what does that matter?"
>
> "It matters because that, too, is what marriage is made of," I told her. "It's balled-up socks and dirty dishes, and whether you sleep with the window open or closed. It's dresser drawers left open or shut, shirts dry cleaned or laundered, dusting behind the bureau or not bothering to. It's choosing between the football game and the ballet. Marriage is the millions of things we do that we must now do together. It is," I said, "work."

of love, I cannot help but remember a man I met in South Africa years ago, an elderly man named Danny, with a crooked back and a scarred face. Denied the vote for most of his life by apartheid, Danny cast his first ballot when he was seventy-three years old. "I waited in a line three kilometers long," he told me. "It was hot and there was no shade. But I had waited for so many years, you know, I wasn't about to leave now. You see," he said, stopping for a moment to draw a deeper breath, "despite her sins, I love my country."

What this woman at Bethany did for her savior was no less the work of love than what Danny did for his country. Her gesture flew in the face of all sense of propriety, proportion, and convention. It was not something designing; she was not looking to please herself or otherwise gain something in return. It was not a transaction. Nor was it measured. In fact, it was the very extravagance of the gesture—what seemed to some to be a pointless waste of a precious resource—that separated it from those feelings that are carefully apportioned out, as though in *their* preciousness they must be used sparingly.

She could not have been a wealthy woman, for what woman of means would have found her way to the house of a leper? So to the charge that she did not know how well that resource might have served the needs of the poor, one can only answer by saying she knew better than most. And in this way her gesture is also an act of self-denial, because by lavishing such an expensive gift the way she did, she was literally taking food out of her own mouth. No, like a tired old man who would stand stooped for hours to cast one vote among millions, or a young mother who would comfort her ailing baby beyond the limits of her own exhaustion, this woman gladly gave what she had for one reason and one reason only: because for her it was an act of pure adoration.

Her love for Jesus was the love a person holds for that which is meaningful beyond anything else she might know, that to which by its very essence one cannot assign a value because to do so is to imply that it could be greater. It transcends logic and defies rationality, and enters instead the world of the ecstatic, by which I mean it is not of the head but of the heart: it does not so much dawn on us as overcome us. Such love is wordless, because words can only point to it, not grasp it. Thus the word *adore*, meaning to "speak to." But not to speak of. It cannot be defined for anyone who has not experienced it and need not be defined for anyone who has.

So, for instance, when on Christmas Eve the faithful gather and sing again the venerable hymn "Adeste Fideles" and our voices swell to the words "O come let us adore him, Christ the lord," our throats clutch and our eyes moisten, and we feel an odd, unsettling warmth in the pit of our stomach. And we silently pledge to ourselves, as we have done every year since we were children, that

this year, *this* year, we will adore him, will live that life of true adoration. And of course we will fall short. But when Lent comes we
will hear this story, of this woman and her gift and of all the terrible and wonderful things that are to follow, and we will be
reminded that the forgiveness we require for having shared our oil
so sparingly will soon be made manifest. And it will speak to us.

## The Risk of Love

When I think of the woman, I think not only of the beauty of what
she did but of the risk, because there is no greater pain in life than to
give ourselves over totally to something unbearably wonderful that
might then be taken from us. It reminds me of the first time I held
my newborn daughter—she was literally two minutes old—and how
suddenly vulnerable I felt, not because I doubted my ability to father
her, but because I so feared what it would be like to somehow lose
her, as parents sometimes do. Fourteen years later we almost did.

When I got the call from my wife that our child had been struck
by a car, those fears came rushing back in an ugly torrent, like a
brutal storm battering a fragile little house. And when we arrived
at her bedside and watched her, comatose, fighting for life, I
remember thinking what absolute joy it would be to trade places
with her—not just that I was willing to do it, but that I would be
thrilled to. And as I began to speak with other parents in similar
situations, I was struck by just how common a revelation this was.
As she has slowly made her way back from her shadowed valley,
I am thankful every day of my life not only for her but for God's
giving me the privilege of knowing in my bones what it feels like
to truly adore another. Such is the work of love.

I believe the woman who served Jesus with nard knew she was
anointing the feet that would soon travel into that shadowed valley, that Jesus would walk it himself and not return, and that he
would do this for her. And so the risk that was thrust upon her was
the risk of pain born of love lost, for much of her love for him was
grounded in his choice to die for her. She loved him so irrationally,
so generously, not only for all he had done in his three short years

of ministry, but also for what he was about to do in his three long days of death. She knew his death would be redemptive, knew that through it she would better come to find God's love of her, of us, knew that in her low estate he loved her no less than had she been of regal bearing and magnificent wealth. And she would suffer the pain of his death because she could do no less, for adoration is not something we decide upon. She could no more choose to adore Jesus than I could choose to adore my newborn child.

## To Love and to Serve

To paraphrase the great Hebrew theologian Martin Buber, adoration does not constitute a state we can live in, but it does constitute a state we cannot live without.[3] When the disciples questioned why the oil was not sold to raise money for the poor, they were reminding themselves that resources are not only too precious but also too poorly distributed to lavish what little we have on ceremonial gestures that put no clothes on the backs of the naked and no food in the bellies of the hungry. And when Jesus responded by telling them, "Let her alone; why do you trouble her? She has done a beautiful thing to me" (Mark 14:6), *he* was reminding them that there are moments in life when love in all its illogical glory breaks in upon us in such a way that we can only stand in awe of it, feel its beauty, and allow it to overwhelm us. And when he then adds, "You always have the poor with you, and whenever you will, you can do good to them," he is further reminding them that the ecstasy of adoration does not obviate the responsibility of service; both, in their own way, constitute the work of love.

In fact, I believe adoration can be a precedent for service, because it provides us with a sense of reverence. I believe that when that woman rose again, and left that house, and entered her world of material need, a world of dusty streets and human want, where lepers hungered for a human touch and children for a piece of bread, she could not help but be transformed. She had experienced the awe of the reverent, what the mystic Rudolf Otto called the *mysterium tremendum et fascinans*—the great mystery, power,

and wonder of God's love.[4] And she knew it was not a love to be
kept close to her breast, hoarded, held for her consumption and
hers alone. As the great Protestant preacher Harry Emerson Fosdick pointed out long ago, we receive God's love the way the Sea
of Galilee receives its source; the water comes in fresh and clean
and wends its way from one end to the other, and then the sea
passes it on, emptying itself into the Jordan River. This way, Fosdick said, the Galilee remains clean and full of life; because it
accepts the water, makes use of it, but then gives it to another.[5]

## Where Will *Our* Inspirations Come From?

In our day and age we have to dig a little deeper than they did two
millennia ago to find the reverence this woman found in the house
of the leper. Our world mitigates against it. There are more people
on earth today than at any time in human history; and yet fewer
heroes come to mind, fewer people who truly inspire reverence in
us. It is telling that in our North American culture our adulation—
and money—is heaped most liberally on professional athletes,
men (and, sadly, only a few women) whose contribution to our
lives is not that they deepen our understanding of the world in
which we live but that for a few short hours they remove us from
it. And if one of them falls from the hero's pedestal we've put him
on because in a drunken stupor he has wrapped his sports car
around a tree or betrayed his wife, a good many of us will prop him
back up there because he can still catch a pass or sink a putt or otherwise stir in us a sense of vicarious glory.

But if we do in fact dig deeper, we may just strike gold, because
while we might lose sight of God, God does not lose sight of us.
Despite the distractions of life that, like gnats at a picnic, seem
small but swirl doggedly around our heads, a reverence for God
and for the truly good in life is there for the one who is patient
enough to believe in it and persistent enough to look for it.

When we think of what might prompt us to reverence, our
minds may drift to the dulcet beauty of Degas's *Beach Landscape*
or the melancholy of Van Gogh's *Potato Eaters*. We may contem-

plate the terse optimism of Emily Dickinson's "The Longest Day" or let the splendor of Brahms's *Requiem* wash over us like a spring rain. But just as easily we could be moved by a riff of Coltrane, the coarse carvings of an Inuit artist, or the studied labors of a child's finger painting, for as Auden said, *every* work of art is rooted in imaginative awe and must be praised for being and for happening.[6] And to the arts some of us could add the inspiration that derives from a truly wonderful sermon, a heartfelt prayer, or the beauty of the holy space in which each is delivered. For my friend Danny, it was the South African ballot box. For my wife and me, it was seeing our daughter find her way back from death's door. For the couple I saw in my office who worked so hard to resurrect their marriage, it was the anniversary they held two years later, when they renewed their vows to one another.

> Do not be conformed to this world but be transformed by the renewal of your mind.
> —Romans 12:2a

But it is not yet enough to be so inspired, because the real challenge is to find a way to make that inspiration endure, coax it forth as we would a shy child, and get it to take root and stay with us despite all the diversions that threaten to chase it away. The challenge is to see the world as I believe that woman who anointed Jesus saw it, transformed. This too is the work of love.

It's work because so much of our time and efforts is given over to things that do not inspire thoughts of the divine, because we have debts to pay and jobs to do, noses to wipe and grudges to harbor, and because ours is not only a secular country but a materialistic one. We are a nation that accords greater status to the movie stars who entertain our children than to the school teachers who educate them. This America of ours, of neon and asphalt, of strip malls and e-baying, of fast food and sitcoms and "reality" shows, does not readily lend itself to the kind of introspection that draws us closer to God. So on a given day we might, say, find ourselves in a hospital or a synagogue, a mosque or maybe a prison or a food pantry, and be moved to tears by an act of breathtaking kindness in which God's love peeks through the pollutions of everyday life.

A flower is given to a lonely woman, a wish is granted to a dying man, a donation is made to an unpopular cause. And then, seconds later, we step outside again where we are barraged by billboards offering us lower mortgages, hair transplants, and a bus ride to the nearest casino. For this reason, among others, love requires so much work, and the quickened pulse we feel from the moment adoration impinges upon us must be nurtured against the intrusions of a culture not naturally disposed to nurturing that moment itself.

And so, when thoughts of Danny come my way, I wonder if today, ten years after he won the right to vote, he is still as impassioned about democracy as he was that hot spring day in April of 1994. I certainly hope so. And I wonder too if the couple who renewed their vows after almost closing the book on their marriage are still enamored enough of one another to find the rare pleasure that only love can offer. And while I do not cease to be grateful beyond words for my daughter's life and health, I wonder too if in time I will come to take it for granted, if my prayers of thanksgiving will become a little less frequent, a little less fervent, and a little more rote, or if my gratitude toward God for this gift will not in time be vitiated by piques of anger over petty things. If that is in fact the case, it will be only because of my own laziness, because I have refused to do the work of love. For as Rilke wrote later in his treatise, "with all our forces gathered close about their lonely, timid, upward beating hearts, *we must learn to love*." And learning is an endeavor of life.

I like to believe it was this way for the woman who anointed Jesus' feet, that she learned lifelong to love. She took the risk of love that day, and did her work, gave all that she had in the name of utter devotion. I choose to believe her life was nothing less than forever changed. As a friend of mine once pointed out about this woman, "she was among the lucky ones, because she came to the table in Simon's home, met him, knelt at his feet, and could look into his eyes. She knew he was real." And then he added, "But then, we know it too, don't we?"

Whether we do or not is up to us. If he is real, it is not that he will be at the table, but that he will be there in the person of the others who are. He is embodied in the ones who have traveled far over rough terrain to be there, from a hardscrabble township in

South Africa or the intensive care unit of a children's hospital. He is there in the ones who tire but do not lose hope. And when they gather, and sit, and rest their weary feet, we may come too and anoint those feet lavishly with that which is most precious in the world. We will anoint them with our gratitude.

2

# The Disciples Fall Asleep at Gethsemane, and the Slave Is Attacked with the Sword

*I am the wound and the knife!*
*I am the blow and the cheek!*
*I am the limbs and the wheel!*
*The victim and the executioner!*

—Baudelaire[1]

*And he came the third time, and said to [his disciples],*
*"Are you still sleeping and taking your rest? It is enough;*
*the hour has come; the Son of man is betrayed into the*
*hands of sinners."*

—Mark 14:41

*And when those who were about him saw what would fol-*
*low, they said, "Lord, shall we strike with the sword?"*
*And one of them struck the slave of the high priest and cut*
*off his right ear. But Jesus said, "No more of this!" And*
*he touched his ear and healed him.*

—Luke 22:49–51

*K*nowing that his time is hastening toward its end, Jesus goes off to do something he has done so often in the past—pray. He seeks out the refuge of Gethsemane that he may be alone to pray. To ensure his solitude, he stations three of his disciples—Peter, James, and John—nearby.

But in a night unlike any other, Jesus, long the paragon of strength to others, falls "on his face and [prays], 'My Father, if it be possible, let this cup pass from me'" (Matt. 26:39).

This was Jesus' time of uncertainty. And it must have been his most grueling hour, in a way more than the hours of pain and humiliation that awaited him, because here he had to wrestle with the demons of his doubts and the temptation to abandon his mission. On the cross, there would be no such temptation. Yet here, where all he wants is quiet, so that he can wrestle with his fears and come to terms with his destiny, he is denied. The disciples don't protect him because they fall asleep, and in short order Jesus is set upon by a crowd better equipped to break up an armed riot than to arrest a lone man who will offer them no resistance. Judas is with them, of course, having led them here, but so are armed guards, ordinary citizens with swords and clubs, slaves, town elders, and surrogates of the priesthood.

Throughout Jesus' ministry people have clamored to press in upon him, to hear his words, to touch his hem, to beg that he touch them so that they might be healed. Even when exhaustion had fallen upon him, when his only desire was to be alone with his thoughts, he did not disappoint; he made himself available to them. And now, when they clamor for his blood, he is there again.

Imagine how he sees his predicament: His disciples, whom he has always watched over and cared for, have failed to watch over him. And so he is surrounded by the angry mob they were to keep at bay. Then, perhaps in a fit of passion or a pang of guilt, one of the disciples—John tells us it is Peter—takes out his knife and severs the ear of a Judean slave. The doubts Jesus has that sent him to the garden cannot have been allayed by this act of brutality committed by someone he has so carefully instructed about the importance of nonviolence. Not only does the disciple carry a weapon, he uses it on another human being. And not only on another human being, but on a slave. His target is not a moneychanger in the temple, or a hypocrite who "tithe[s] mint and rue and every herb, and neglect[s] justice and the love of God" (Luke 11:42). He is not a tax collector, usurer, or envoy of dreaded Rome. Though Jesus deplored violence exacted on any person, from any walk of life, his disappointment could only have been deepened by Peter's assault on one of the lowest stature, who has no freedoms, holds no status, owns no goods, and enjoys no privileges.

It is an extraordinary moment when the disciple is rebuked and the slave is made whole. Consider first Jesus' response to Peter: According to Matthew, Jesus tells the disciple that "all who take the sword will perish by the sword" (Matt. 26:52). A man who has journeyed with Jesus for his entire ministry, the rock upon whom his church will soon be built, still doesn't get it and still has to be sternly reminded, as he must have been reminded on so many occasions, of the futility of violence either as a preemptive or a retributive gesture.

By comparison, consider Jesus' response to the slave: he, a man who is a part of the crowd and who no doubt has no affection for Jesus, let alone allegiance to him, is the recipient of Jesus' last earthly miracle. So here too is Jesus ever the healer: the slave's beliefs have no bearing on whether or not he has the right to be whole.

> "For hatred can never put an end to hatred. Only love can."
> —Buddha[2]

Anticipating that his own blood will soon be shed both by and for this crowd, Jesus offers them this one gesture of unexpected kindness. And by it he tells them that when that church does come into being and people recall his wondrous works, they will recall as well that, in what may have been the last of these works, he offered perhaps his most important lesson. He demonstrated that God's love is not confined to those who claim him to be their Christ, but is universal. It knows no bounds of sectarianism or faith, no creed or doctrine, no nation of origin, no sexual orientation. It can be claimed by no one as his or her own exclusive purview.

## There Are No Commoners, No Kings and Queens

Because God's love is so generously given, it is apt that the target of Peter's wrath and Jesus' love is a lowly slave. Who better for Jesus to touch than a slave whose history is as modest as his? Years earlier, God's love had come into the world in a manger, a wooden box that held the food and detritus of lowly animals, and chances are that at about the same time that slave was born in conditions not much different. For both men and for their families, the world was a small but dangerous place that offered little security and much heartache. Neither would ever know great wealth, and both would see the excesses of those who did. Jesus did not necessarily share a set of beliefs with this man, but he did share something far more precious: As products of their life's circumstances, both could understand how easily we are wounded and how rarely we are healed.

So just as Mary was common enough to receive the annunciation, shepherds to be the first to see the child, and a poor beggar like Bartimaeus to receive the gift of sight (Mark 10:46), this slave was common enough to bear the message that God's love is not confined to those who receive it through one story and not another. Jesus did not want to make the slave promise to become his follower. He did not even want to make him confess that he believed in God. He simply wanted to make him well. A gesture of wondrous promise and daunting challenge.

His action is a promise, for *it* assures us that God's love leaves none of us behind; it unites all humanity in a way that is bigger than anything that might divide us. And it is daunting for exactly the same reason—because it means that God's love extends to people we regard as our enemies or do not regard at all. It means that we must come to terms with the fact that God loves everyone—the mean-spirited, the stingy, the dishonest. It means God loves the politician who abuses his power and the parent who abuses hers, the road rager and the drug dealer, the pimp and the punk. He loves the smug and the self-centered, the inveterate criminal and the incurable racist. And, more to the point, Jesus' action means that we must decide what it means for us to sheathe the sword of self-righteousness and to love them too; to object to the people we find objectionable but to find it in our hearts to care about them as well. As George Bernard Shaw pointed out, "the worst sin toward our fellow creatures is . . . to be indifferent to them: that's the essence of inhumanity."[3] It's hard to think compassionately about the welfare of those we don't know or don't like; it's easy to regard them with indifference. But to do so is to surrender our humanity; to affirm that humanity is to remember that beyond all that separates us, there is one thing that is fundamental to all of us: We are all sinners, all in need of love, of grace, of forgiveness.

When Jesus said that those who live by the sword will die by it, he meant that peace is possible only when we learn to look at one another not as adversaries but as human beings who have the same needs and harbor the same hopes as we. In this, he excluded *no* one; and so that night he was speaking not just to the disciple who pulled his knife, but to all of those who had come with fire in their eyes, weapons in their hands, and hatred in their hearts. They not only came to arrest him; they somehow relished it. That hatred was visceral, as it so often is. Once having identified him as their enemy, they did not simply want justice done; they wanted their blood lust satisfied. They lived by the sword, at least in this moment; the only way they could countenance this lust was by seeing Jesus not as a person, but as an enemy. And they would die by their sword, if only metaphorically, because their actions would only diminish them as human beings.

I believe that at another time in his life, perhaps on another day like today, this slave knew what it meant to hate: He woke up ill one morning, but his master summoned him nonetheless. Before he had anything to eat, he was told to prepare breakfast for this man's family, or to run and deliver a message to someone in another part of town, or perhaps to go and fetch the master's concubine and slip her into his chambers undetected. Every day he does his chores without complaining, but he receives neither acknowledgment nor pay. His master does not ask about his health or the health of his children, does not recognize the hardship of this man's life, perhaps degrades him in front of others, and does not think twice about sending him off to a garden on the outskirts of Jerusalem in the dead of night to help arrest a man with whom he has no quarrel.

I believe that at such a time, that slave could hate, could actually physically desire, above all earthly pleasures, that his master's life be changed from manored privilege to utter calamity. The slave could hate in this way because his master's inhumanity toward him induced in him an identical feeling of inhumanity toward his master.

## The Spiral of Violence

When we fail to see or to respect the other person's humanity, we set in motion a terrible series of events that spiral us downward, as through Dante's circles, to a hellish place where we are overtaken only by our basest of emotions. We no longer believe that she has the same blood coursing through her veins as we do, or that he has been profoundly shaped by the circumstances of his life just as we have. We can't imagine that, had our circumstances been less different, we could even have been friends. Instead, violence ensues, and then envelops.

I am reminded of a story from the 1991 Gulf War. Iraqi troops were in full retreat out of Kuwait and were headed back toward Baghdad via whatever means they had at their disposal. Some were in tanks, some in cars, some on foot. American fighter jets were in hot pursuit, firing their weapons indiscriminately and killing thousands of men, many of whom first entered the military not voluntarily but with a gun to their heads. What was supposed to be restrained retaliatory targeting on the part of the airmen soon became an exercise in carnage. When it was over, the road to Baghdad became known as the highway of death, and one particularly exultant airman was quoted as saying, "You should've seen it out there; it was like a video game. We aim,we shoot, they fall. It was awesome!" Upon returning to base to reload, all the young man wanted to do was get back up in the air and kill some more.

The airman could view this carnage as "awesome" because to the air crews those soldiers on the ground were no longer human beings. They had become, in the grotesque vernacular of the pilot, nothing more than dots of light on a darkened screen; alien invaders neutralized by staccato clicks on the joystick, a few hundred here, a few hundred there, until the screen flashes "Game Over" and the hero totes his final score, belying Whitman's lament that when "my enemy is dead, a man divine as myself is dead."[4]

Ethicist Donald Shriver, reflecting on the experience of the American military in the Gulf War, offered a postscript:

> When relief crews hit the ground to assess the damage, one of the scenes they came upon was a dead soldier who was clinging to a cardboard box. In the box was a girl's dress, new, with the tags still on it. Maybe he stole it, I don't know. But that doesn't matter. What came to mind for me was that this was a man who had a daughter or a niece or a sister back home, and who was looking forward to returning to that family. And giving the little girl perhaps the first dress she would ever own. This guy was a soldier who did the bidding of a horrific regime. But he was also a human being, whose loss would touch other human beings. Including a young child who would not understand why he never came home.[5]

Again, Whitman, on viewing the remains of a Civil War dead:

> Young man I think I know you—
> I think this face is the face of the Christ himself,
> Dead and divine and brother of us all, and here again he lies.[6]

The violence in the air that night in Gethsemane, not unlike the violence of war, was a beast born into a waiting world. Spawned by fear, birthed by hatred, and nurtured by ignorance, it consumed everything in its path for no reason other than that this consumption kept it alive. Which is why Jesus healed the slave—because as they would all learn in a few short days, only love is powerful enough to fell the beast.

## Other Than, Not Better Than

When violence is the rejection by one person of another's humanity, it can take forms as blatant as a gun or as subtle as an attitude. A family moves in to a new town, only to find their neighbors giving them wide berth; keeping their distance, because this new family is somehow different. Perhaps it is their nationality or the color of their skin; or perhaps they are a family in which both parents are of the same sex. No one throws rocks through their windows or burns crosses on their lawns, but no one extends themselves either, and in a neighborhood of potluck suppers and tag sales they feel conspicuously left out. And so the neighbors never learn that this is a family of wonderful people, whose kids could be lifelong friends with theirs or whose adults are people of great wit, wisdom, and generosity. "Do not neglect to show hospitality to strangers," wrote the author of the book of Hebrews, *"for thereby some have entertained angels unawares"* (13:2). That this might have been a family of earthly angels is a possibility that remains unexamined, right up to the time when, feeling the sting of rejection, they sell their home and go elsewhere. They suffer for the ignorance of others, but the ignorant suffer for it too, because that ignorance only perpetuates the narrowness of their judgment and the pettiness of their thought. They live by the sword of their prejudice, and they die by it.

It is a sense of superiority, of course, that sustains this kind of violence. Peter thought he was superior to the mob, just as the American fighter pilots thought they were superior to their Iraqi enemy, and just as those of us who discriminate against others do so because we think we are somehow better than they. And while we are at no loss to find other examples of this kind of thinking in our troubled world, one of its most dangerous incarnations occurs among those of us who believe, as Peter may have believed that night, that God is theirs, to the exclusion of others. This is the stuff of which wars are waged, friendships strained, and families torn asunder.

I don't pretend to be a historian, but I don't believe I have ever lived through a time of greater religious intolerance than the time we live in now. Christian denominations are at odds within their own ranks over social issues that bear great theological weight. One camp believes the church has become libertine and another that it has become reactionary. One hews close to a literal understanding of the Bible and another to the expansive possibilities of interpretation. Some camps—whether conservative or liberal—believe politics and religion should not mix, and others can't imagine how religion cannot be brought to bear on matters of war and peace, economic and gender injustice, or the creeping colonialism of the last remaining superpower. Differences have always existed. What is so chilling now, however, is the entrenchment of these views and the general unwillingness to seek common ground or respect those differences.

To this we can add the great schisms that persist, say, between supporters of Israel and Palestine, where some on each side believe the only way for their state to exist in peace is for the other to not exist at all. Nor is the standoff all that different in Ireland, where for some Protestants and Catholics religion is an excuse for the venom each holds for the other. And perhaps nowhere is there a greater gulf of mistrust than between radical Islam and the West, where the most strident among Muhammad's followers see Western culture as materially decadent and spiritually vapid, and the most strident Westerners see Islam as a primitive, misogynistic, and violent religion.

> "Suffering follows an evil thought as the wheel of the cart follows the oxen that draw it."
> —Buddha[7]

Because we leave ourselves no room for conversation, an avoidable tragedy becomes a near inevitability. We cannot talk about those issues that divide us because we are unwilling to believe there is truth in what the other person—or group, or nation—might have to say. Some years ago I counseled a couple who would get into arguments that they could not find their way out of, and this situation really frustrated them. After listening to the postmortems on some of these arguments, I realized that what plagued them plagues the world. I told them what I thought I saw going on.

"We enter disputes looking to do one of three things," I said. "We decide that we want either to inflict pain on the other person (and we all know what buttons to push), to have our opinion prevail, or to reach some compromise and accommodation. And whatever approach we take will be the one that prevails. In a real sense, the fates of your arguments are decided before the first salvo is launched." For these folks it was all about winning and losing, which in most cases meant that the resolution of one disagreement was laying the seeds for the next one.

And so it is with quarrels of any kind; when little ground is ever given, common ground is never reached. Voices of reason are lost in the noise of recrimination, and it is impossible for us to move closer to another when our heels are dug in. Only when we begin by recognizing that maybe, just maybe, there is some truth in what the other person has to say—or at least some shred of information that will help *us* understand better why they believe what they believe—can the seeds of community be planted.

## Swords into Plowshares

In the end I'm glad Peter did what he did, because I'm glad Jesus did what *he* did. Peter's act of intolerance gave Jesus one last opportunity to teach anyone who would listen that violence is a bad way to live and a sure way to die. With this one gesture he told them all that the old ways would no longer work. He told his adversaries, the ones with the clubs and the spears, that no one can be a perpetrator of violence without eventually becoming a victim of it as well. He told his disciples that when he is gone they must stay awake, alert, vigilant, and attentive, because people will try to disrupt the work he has charged them to do, the work of bringing love and tolerance to loveless and intolerant places. And by healing a slave he told them all that this love does not honor boundaries, that it is not the rule of one group over another, that it is poured out as freely for those who claim nothing for themselves as it is for those who claim everything. To paraphrase the author of the epistle to the Galatians, there is neither Jew nor Greek, there is neither slave or free, there is neither male nor female, for we are *all* heirs to the promise (Gal. 3:28).

As heirs to Paul's promise perhaps we would do well to sheathe our swords, pound them into plowshares, and with those plowshares till the battlefields of this earth, for these are our common grounds. Perhaps the dirt once stained in blood would then churn rich and dark and brown, breathe, and break apart beneath that great blade. And perhaps we could plant the seeds of humility and hope and nurture them, that they might grow skyward, ascend into the heavens. And perhaps all this would be pleasing to God.

# Caiaphas

*There is no greater heresy than that the office sanctifies the holder of it.*

—Lord Acton[1]

*Then the chief priests and the elders of the people gathered in the palace of the high priest, who was called Caiaphas, and took counsel together in order to arrest Jesus by stealth and kill him. But they said, "Not during the feast, lest there be a tumult among the people."*

—Matthew 26:3–5

The story of Caiaphas is timeless, because it is the story of any person who is entrusted with power to serve the common good but uses it to satisfy his or her own pleasures. In this regard he is the precursor to the revolutionary who displaces a despot only to become one himself, the priest who takes sexual advantage of children in his charge, even the older brother who makes life miserable for his younger sister. He could just as easily have been of any other faith or no faith at all, could have been a tax collector or a landlord, could have been a senator or a king; it doesn't matter. What matters is that he was the kind of person for whom, as Acton also said, power corrupts and absolute power corrupts absolutely.

## The High Priests

Caiaphas was part of an aristocracy, much like modern royal families. He did nothing to earn his position, for, like royalty, the priesthood was hereditary. With it came extraordinary privileges: rank, wealth, influence, and limited, exclusive membership in the vocational order, the ultimate in nepotism. Most important, priests served as mediators between the human and the divine, and because they were thought to be closer to God than everyone else, they alone performed ritual sacrifices, interpreted signs and auguries, did what they thought necessary to preserve a theocratic state, and dispensed wisdom on legal matters, all in the name of serving God's interests on earth. In other words, by mere accident of birth, priests could claim superior wealth, breeding, insight, and power over the people they were anointed to look after. And for the high priest, like a king among dukes, the undeserved sense of superiority was even greater.

It doesn't take a great leap of imagination then to understand that a man like Caiaphas, empowered by the office and its trappings, would be in no hurry to relinquish them. Nor is it hard to imagine that Caiaphas could become so intoxicated with the glitter and power of his position that he would completely lose sight of the fact that they were intended not to meet his desires but to help him better fulfill the mandates of his God and the needs of his people. Giving unchecked power to any human being always raises the possibility of abuse of that which has been entrusted to them.

So abuse he did, as evidenced by the fact that he saw in Jesus such a threat that, by Mark's account, he not only wanted him dead but wanted it done quickly and quietly because "he feared the people." To put it another way, in Caiaphas's eyes, Jesus' message carried just enough authority to be dangerous. It was dangerous not because it blasphemed God—against which Caiaphas would naturally have taken issue—but, quite the contrary, because it presented a kind of divine love that could bring hope to the oppressed masses. That love, he feared, could incite those masses to want a freer and more dignified life, and if their desire angered the empire it could cost Caiaphas his job, trappings and all.

If Caiaphas had been the least bit introspective or self-aware, in Jesus he might have seen himself as if reflected in a mirror—oddly similar but completely opposite. Both men were products of their religious lineage, both parsed the Scriptures for the people, both invited controversy as emissaries of God, both stirred fear in some and fealty in others. Yet one possessed nothing but his integrity, and the other possessed everything but his integrity.

## Serving God or Serving Self?

We cannot simultaneously do God's work and fight God's will. In the America of the1960s and early '70s, caught up in a terrible and terribly unpopular war in southeast Asia, the word *pacification* made its way into popular speech. The term, perhaps best embodied in the war strategies of General William Westmoreland, the war's military mastermind, referred to a war tactic that journalist Peter Arnett described—without a trace of irony—as a willingness to destroy a village in order to save it.[2] What he meant was that as a tool of war we could obliterate entire villages in the name of protecting the very people we were rendering homeless and landless. This Orwellian notion isn't far from what lay behind Caiaphas's efforts to silence Jesus; in the name of protecting the people whose welfare he was sacredly sworn to attend to, he schemed to remove from their midst one man who, as a teacher and a healer, could offer them limitless care, the likes of which they had never known.

Caiaphas, like Westmoreland, made himself an easy target, a guy who rejected the relationship between the privilege of power and the responsibility to wield it honorably. When he assumed the priesthood, he partook in a centuries-old ritual of consecration in which he swore to embrace the duties of his office, to comport himself in the likeness of God, to live a life of sanctity in the service of God, to do his work *in God's name.* The ceremony stressed the obligations of the office, not the opportunities it afforded the officeholder. And in fact one premise of the priesthood was the higher the station, the greater the responsibilities, and therefore the greater the humility that was expected of the one who ascended to it. For what is more humbling than representing God to your people, a responsibility bestowed on you, not because you are qualified for it, but because you are called to it?

In the ceremony of consecration that marked Caiaphas's ordination into the priesthood, the celebrant would take the blood of a sacrificed animal and, as Moses had done with Aaron thousands of years earlier, perform a rite unique to Judaism. He would first dab the blood on the side of Caiaphas's ear, then on his right hand, and finally on a toe on his right foot. The historian Philo would later explain, "Those consecrated for the priesthood must be pure in words, actions, and in his whole life. Words are judged by hearing, the hand is the symbol of action, and the foot is the pilgrimage of life."[3] And as Rabbi Joseph Hertz expanded on Philo's explanation in his own *Torah Commentary*, "the ear was touched with blood, that it may be consecrated to hear the word of God; the hand, to perform the duties of the priesthood; and the foot, to walk the path of righteousness."[4]

These are the qualities of character that God requires for us to do his will: When we serve God, we first listen to God, even if it means hearing things we do not want to hear. We then take what we have heard and act on it, even if it means doing so at great personal cost. And from there we go forth; we make our lifelong pilgrimage of faith, and we do so humbly, even as it takes us to places where we are not welcome, not popular, not safe, places where our direction is unsure and our future is uncertain. We go out, as Whitman said, "joyously on trackless seas, fearless for unknown shores."[5] This is what was expected of the priests, but as in any community believing itself special in the eyes of God, it was what was expected of everyone.

I believe Caiaphas abused his authority because he loved it too much. He so valued it and the things that it brought him that, like Westmoreland in his Vietnam adventurism, he sacrificed the principles of his office to protect the powers that derived from it. The priesthood was his sacred calling, but blinded by temptations, Caiaphas lost sight of his true calling, which is, as Micah observed, "to do justice, and to love kindness, and to walk humbly with your God" (Mic. 6:8).

When I think of Caiaphas, I think of what Harry Truman said in 1945 when Franklin Roosevelt died. Truman had become the most powerful man on earth during the deadliest war in modern history.

Instead of feeling flush with his new power, he was awed by the responsibility to wield it properly (whether he did so or not is another matter). Said Truman, "There have been few men in all history the equal of the man into whose shoes I am stepping. I pray God I can measure up to the task." And then later (to reporters) Truman added, "Boys, if you ever pray, pray for me now. I don't know whether you fellows ever had a load of hay fall on you, but when they told me yesterday what had happened, it felt like the moon, the stars and all the planets had fallen on me."[6] For Truman, power was a weight on his shoulders; for Caiaphas, it was a toy at his fingertips.

## A Little Caiaphas in All of Us, a Lot of Him in Some of Us

In my own life I have, I'm afraid, seen more of Caiaphas than Truman in my flirtations—however small—with power. I remember, for example, the first time I preached a sermon at Riverside Church, and how heady an experience it was. The sanctuary is enormous, a city block in length, a hundred feet from floor to ceiling, with seating for 2,500 people. It is ornate, adorned with magnificent statuary, embellished by Tiffany windows. The pulpit, of carved stone, rises above the congregation and is capped by a magnificent wood canopy two stories high.

As I began that first Sunday to speak from that pulpit high above the congregation, I wanted them to know that I was merely a vessel of God, a mouthpiece for his word. In reality, however, I could not help but sense a rush of energy as I stood there and spoke; and while I'd like to say it was the Holy Spirit that I felt, it was nothing more than my own ego, delighted to be standing where men and women far greater than I had stood. I felt vicariously important, and no worse infirmity can visit a preacher at a time like that than a sense of importance. Where I was supposed to be emptying myself to God, I was filling myself with pride. Where I was supposed to be letting God speak through me, I was hoping instead that the congregation would be impressed by my

This is a fable of a church rich in prestige but poor in purpose: A tattered, thread-bare old man entered the great sanctuary of the very prominent church and was greeted by an usher. He went to hug the usher, who mildly rebuked him, saying, "We don't do that here, sir." The usher then sat the man down in the backmost pew, even though there were empty seats closer to the front. "You will be more comfortable back here," he said to the man. When the service started and the preacher began to preach, the old man stood up and said gleefully, "Praise God and preach the word, brother!" at which point the usher came over to him and explained to him, "We do not care for outbursts like that here, sir." The chas-tened old man sat down, then got up, and asked the usher, "Is this God's house?" The usher replied, "Why, yes, of course it is." "Okay," said the old man, as he began to leave, "I'll come back some time when he's home."

words and dazzled by my style. I was not ministering *in God's name*, but in my own.

I can't recall much about the content of my sermon, but I do remember that it was delivered on August 6, Hiroshima Day, when we commemorate the dropping of the first atomic bomb on a civil-ian city and pray for both the living and the dead. I also remember castigating Harry Truman for having done such a craven thing as ordering that the bomb be dropped. I would criticize him similarly today, because the slaughter of the innocents that ensued from that one act is inexcusable in civilized society, but I'd like to believe that today I would be addressing Truman not as preacher to sinner but as sinner to sinner.

It wasn't the first time, nor was it the last, that I let my ego get the better of me in my work. When I reflect upon that sort of behav-ior, I do well to think back to what Melanie Morrison, a colleague and truly gifted minister, said about the sin of pride: "Always remember your ordination, because when you accepted the call to do God's work, you were *on your knees*." She was right of course; we do our highest work, or, more to the point, we do God's high-est work, when we are brought low.

While it's a hazard of my profession in particular, it's not as though only some of us fall prey to what Nietzsche called our will to power. In politics it cost Richard Nixon the presidency and his place in history, and in sports it cost Pete Rose his place in the baseball Hall of Fame. In battle Napoleon paid by losing Moscow, and in business multimillionaire stock trader Michael Milken paid by losing both his freedom (he spent two years in prison) and his reputation.

The bully who beats his classmate, the husband who beats his wife, the insouciant heir to her daddy's fortune, all have a dose of that arrogance as well, insofar as their awareness of the power at their disposal is matched only by their ignorance as to how they are supposed to use it. What is true for a preacher in the pulpit is true for anyone else, in any walk of life, who ever exercises power either for the welfare or the detriment of others: We have a very different view of our world when we stand above it from when we kneel before it.

## Love, Devotion, Surrender

To live as if we are on our knees, to live disposed to the doing of God's will, means not only being prepared to take on certain challenges, but being prepared to surrender certain comforts and sureties as well.

When I look for a symbol of this kind of surrender, I think of Pat Tillman. Pat was an exceedingly gifted and well-paid football player for the Arizona Cardinals. Young and talented, he had a bright future, but he left the team, the considerable paycheck, and the profession to become a member of the elite Army Rangers. Both his pay and his life expectancy dropped precipitously, but for Tillman it was a matter of serving his country in a way that was consistent with his beliefs, rather than playing a game simply because he had a talent for it. And in the end, Tillman gave up his life in an Afghanistan war zone.

Although many don't share Tillman's belief that the military holds the answer for much of what ails America, and some would rather have had him join VISTA, or Habitat for Humanity, or the War Resisters League, we must credit him for hewing to his beliefs and making the ultimate sacrifice for those beliefs. Most professional athletes are not heroes, nor is every soldier a hero, but there is real heroism in someone who is willing to live by principles rather than platitudes; and when the time comes to pay a price for those principles, I admire a person who is willing to do just that.

To the ranks of the heroic I would add Jennifer Casolo, a bright young woman who grew up with some means and graduated with honors from Brandeis University. Jennifer could have parlayed her degree into high-paying work but instead in the 1980s she dedicated herself to the cause of justice in El Salvador—not a popular or particularly safe battle in the days of U.S.-sponsored repression there. Jennifer was imprisoned for her efforts, but since her release continues to work on behalf of the rights of the poor and politically dispossessed of Central America.

And for all the Pat Tillmans and Jennifer Casolos we hear about, there are countless more we do not: There is the couple in Harlem who have poured their time, their labors, and their money into founding the Harlem Little League, so that kids in a tough urban area can have the chance to play "America's game." And the husband and wife in suburban Detroit who gave up their high-paying jobs because they couldn't abide their tax dollars going to support the nuclear arms race, and decided to live lives of material simplicity instead. Or the young heir apparent to his father's media empire who, after gratefully acknowledging to his parents the life of privilege he had enjoyed growing up, became an inner-city public school teacher and lived in a modest apartment not far from his students.

The anti-Caiaphases are alive and well, and dwell among us. They are in churches and synagogues and mosques and schools, on playgrounds and in classrooms. They are organizing underpaid workers in Mexican maquiladoras and treating undernourished children in Rwandan clinics, negotiating for peace between L.A. gangs and advocating for the just treatment of prisoners in places like Belfast, Beirut, and Baltimore. They are at work in the fields of the Lord, where the pay is scant, the hours are long, and the rewards are beyond measure.

But of course virtually any calling can lend itself to doing the work of the Lord, not just Caiaphas's. He could have enjoyed the wealth and power that were his due and applied them to improving the material and spiritual lives of his people. He could have represented his people before the Roman authorities and made their case for safer roads, more autonomy, more respect for Jewish traditions, and a fairer distribution of resources. He could have preached patience and perseverance to his people, reminding them that although they were an occupied nation, they were a proud one. He could have, as Kipling said, walked among them and shown the common touch, could have punished any colleague who brought dishonor on the priesthood, and could have seen to it that the poorest of the poor were adequately fed, clothed, and sheltered.

Caiaphas was a stunning success and a miserable failure. True, he held his job for eighteen years, longer than any man who preceded or succeeded him to the throne. But if the purpose of his job was to invite hope into the lives of the Jewish community he was sworn to serve, if it was to govern that community with compassion seasoned with wisdom, if it was to know God's will and do God's work on behalf of that community and at all costs, then he truly failed. And so he was the mirror image of Christ. His sin is what he did with his power; his tragedy is what he *could have done* with it.

## One Final Note

Unfortunately, one last legacy of Caiaphas makes him even more dangerous in death than in life. He is depicted as the one leading the conspiracy to have Jesus arrested (Matt. 26), and because, as John reminds his readers, "it was Caiaphas who had given counsel to the Jews that it was expedient that one man should die for the people" (18:14), his story is still used by anti-Semites to fuel their bigotry. Because he was a leader of the Jews, he is often held up by bigots as the embodiment of Judaism. But we must remember that his story is his alone. He is not emblematic of Jews or Judaism any more than Pat Robertson's sclerotic fundamentalism is emblematic of the beliefs of all Christians or Osama bin Laden's obsession with the nobility of suicide is shared by all Muslims. Caiaphas does not represent a race or a creed or a people; he represents a human condition—the thirst for power and the unwillingness to do right by it. That is all. And that is enough.

# The Riddle of Peter

*Once to every life and nation comes the moment to decide,
in the strife of Truth with Falsehood, for the good or evil
side.*

— James Russell Lowell[1]

*And Jesus said to them, "You will all fall away; for it is
written, 'I will strike the shepherd, and the sheep will be
scattered.' But after I am raised up, I will go before you to
Galilee." Peter said to him, "Even though they all fall
away, I will not." And Jesus said to him, "Truly, I say to
you, this very night, before the cock crows twice, you will
deny me three times."*

—Mark 14:27–30

## First among Equals

From the minutiae to the momentous the Gospels afford us a fuller
picture of Peter than of any of the other disciples. We know, for
instance, that he was a common laborer who made his living fish-
ing the waters of Galilee. We know that when Jesus called him to
follow him, he dropped his net and did so. We also know that he
was the *first* of the Twelve to be called, a distinction he no doubt
wore as a badge of honor and a burden of great responsibility: first
among equals.

It is to Peter's house that Jesus returns after preaching his Sermon on the Mount, and, later, it is Peter's boat that Jesus miracu-
lously fills with "a great shoal of fish" (Luke 5:6). Later still, when

the disciples are adrift at sea in the midst of a terrible storm, with Jesus urging them to set foot upon the water and walk to him, it is Peter alone who dares to do so. It was his courage that propelled him, just as it was his fear when, nearing Jesus but feeling the force of the wind in his face, he panicked and had to be rescued from drowning. "O man of little faith, why did you doubt?" Jesus asks (Matt. 14:31), but one can only wonder what enormous reservoirs of faith it took to step foot out of that boat in the first place, to leave the safety of a harbor and sail into unknown waters and uncertain fate.

And in a moment that would forever shape the course of Christian history, it was Peter who first saw in Jesus the person who was to come to be known as the Son of God.

Jesus had brought the Twelve to a place called Caesarea Philippi, a beautiful, naturally luxuriant setting high above sea level and overlooking the fertile Jordan Valley. By now they had seen him perform miracles, feed multitudes, heal the sick, and preach with extraordinary authority and insight. His reputation was growing. But so was the peril around him; the rumblings of discontent were no longer far off, and the disciples still weren't clear as to what was going to happen.

Perhaps Jesus sensed the uncertainty in them, and perhaps he also sensed that his time was running out. If his work was going to continue after his death, it would fall to them to carry the load, and so he needed to know that they understood the full measure of his ministry.

With this in mind he poses a question. "Who do people say that I am?" he asks, and, like school kids caught unawares for a pop quiz, they give it their best guess.

"Some say John the Baptist, others say Elijah, and others Jeremiah or one of the prophets" (Matt. 16:14), they tell him, eagerly, if unconvincingly.

Jesus then presses the issue: "But who do *you* say that I am?" at which point all but one fall silent. Peter stands up, looks at him, and tells him with utter conviction, "You are the Christ, the Son of the living God" (Matt. 16:16). If the Gospel accounts are correct, it is the first time these words are uttered, and their gravitas is not wasted on Jesus. "You are Peter," he tells his first chosen, "and on this rock I will build my church" (Matt. 16:18). In other words, because the first among equals was also the first to have seen in Jesus something truly godly, it is he who is anointed to become the first leader of the postresurrection era.

And according to the book of Acts, that is precisely what Peter became: the rock on which the early church was built. Not long after Jesus' death, he alone stood before "the brethren," it records, and directed them to select a twelfth disciple to replace Judas Iscariot. They obeyed, choosing a man named Matthias, a man he had personally presented to them. At Pentecost—a Jewish harvest festival commonly called the Feast of the Weeks—Peter's preaching is said to have been so powerful that it converted three thousand souls to the new faith. There are even miracles ascribed to him, as it is said that he healed the lame outside the temple gates. If any one person can be credited with serving as a still point in the turning world that was the early church, it would be Peter, and one is left to wonder what might have been the fate of that little band, had not this first among them stepped out from their midst and led them into the uncertain, perilous world of persecution and hope.

## Toward Denial and Doubt

But still there is that shadow of cowardice that looms over his legacy. Of all the people who might have denied knowing Jesus that fateful night, why Peter?

It was Maundy Thursday. The Feast of the Passover. Jesus' last night before his death. Clouds of intrigue brewed around him, followers fell by the wayside, and enemies pressed in upon him. Smelling the danger in the air, Peter, unsolicited, pledged his fealty—as he had on other occasions—promising to follow Jesus even to death, regardless of what the others did.

He no doubt meant it too; there is no evidence anywhere prior or subsequent that Peter was anything but wholly committed to the one he called the Christ. This, after all, is a man who left his family, his work, his home, and his village to follow a Nazarene teacher of no repute. He had long ago given up what comforts he had for the wholly uncomfortable prospect of a world of itinerancy and hardship. So why, after all this, would this one man—the first called, the only one to have known Jesus' true identity as the Son of God—now deny knowing him at all? Why did he, of all people, succumb to what Dorothy Dix called "the dark power of the future"?[2]

The answer, perhaps, is because it *had to be Peter*. He is the most likely culprit because he is the least likely. True, it could have been any of the others. Indeed it may have been—we have no way of knowing who else was put to the test that night, and Jesus does not tell Peter that he *alone* would deny his allegiance. But it has to have been Peter, because if the one of great faith is capable of great treachery, then anyone of lesser faith is as well. If Peter is to be the rock, the precursor, the cornerstone, and the embodiment of the Christian church that was yet to come, then he had to be—as he had been in that boat upon the stormy sea—one for whom courage tugs at one end of his heart and fear tugs at the other. In other words, to say that Peter could deny Jesus is to say that any one of us—if not of lesser faith then surely not of greater—is capable of doing the same. Peter is all of us, is each of us, is any of us. The rock is also the reminder that as the fellowship of believers we are an imperfect lot.

## The Allure of the Known

We don't want this of Peter, of course. Our heroes represent the highest of our aspirations, and we want them to do so with moral impeccability. We don't want to learn that our favorite athlete abuses drugs or the neighborhood cop is on the take. We want our movie stars to be as daring and generous offscreen as they are on, and our politicians to govern with the same integrity as the Constitution they swear to uphold. We want our clergy—the descendants of Peter—to practice what they preach and exercise the same moral rectitude they advocate, especially when it comes to ministering to our children. We don't want moral ambiguity; we want certainty. But, as André Gide warned, "Believe those who are seeking the truth; doubt those who find it."[3]

In our hunger for perfection we are like the tragic protagonist in Thomas Mann's *Death in Venice,* who is obsessed by the striking beauty of a young Polish boy he views from a distance. The old man idealizes the child in his mind and pursues him with singleness of purpose, but instead of a human being, the child is—in the man's eyes—the incarnation of a flawless, impossible ideal. As if afraid that reality might vitiate his fantasy, he never actually approaches the child but instead worships him from afar. "All his care was not to lose sight of the figure after which his eyes thirsted,"[4] wrote Mann.

But perfection being, in Paul's words, "not a thing to be grasped," it not only eluded the man but ultimately cost him his life, for when forced to choose between leaving Venice to avoid certain illness (the city was beset by cholera) and staying to feed his obsession, he chose to stay. It is an apt and timeless metaphor; perfection being an illusion, the pursuit of it can lead us only to disillusionment and despair.

So perhaps there is this allowance in the choice of Peter to embody the church. Jesus did not conceive of a perfect man to do the job, because the church would not be—could not be—a perfect institution. It would instead be a gathering of redeemed sinners, of people who, in the safety of a community perched far above the woes of the world, would find it easy to recognize Jesus as their Christ but who, when danger lurks in difficult days, might find it just as easy to deny they even knew him.

In April of 1968, the Easter season, the city of Louisville, Kentucky, found itself in the grips of some difficult days of its own. After years of racial segregation and the disenfranchisement of blacks by whites, the city was simmering with resentment and fear triggered by the assassination of Dr. Martin Luther King. Seeking some form of redress for their grievances, a small group of black men and women decided to take their concerns to some of the city's more prominent white citizens. They did this one Sunday morning by gathering outside the doors of the Harvey Browne Presbyterian Church, one of Louisville's most prominent white congregations.

Shortly before the first of two services ended, the group gathered in a circle and began singing songs of Christian protest. Their action was peaceful, but disturbing and dramatic. "It was as though they were reminding us that if we would not leave our pews and engage the struggle that threatened to divide our city, the struggle would come to us," recalled Nancy Combs, a classmate of mine and one of the parishioners in attendance that day.

When, at the service's end, senior minister Joe Mullin heard the singing, he took off his robes and announced to his congregation, "Especially in light of the death of Dr. King, I cannot in good conscience remain in here when this is going on out there. Anyone who wishes to join me is certainly welcome." And with that, in a gesture that some said ultimately cost him his job, Mullin went out those front doors and joined in the protest. In this one event the congregation became, if you will, the embodiment of the church, the paradox that is Peter. There was no logic, however tortured, to justify the treatment blacks received in Louisville or anywhere else in America. And the people in the sanctuary that Sunday, good Christians schooled in their Scriptures, knew theirs was a just God who does not favor one group of people over another. They knew that in Leviticus God instructed, "you shall not oppress your neighbor" (19:13), that in Matthew Jesus reminded his followers, "Whatever you would wish [others] would do to you, do so to them" (7:12), and that in Acts Peter himself observed, "Truly I perceive that God shows no partiality" (10:34). But more than this, they knew in their very bones what was right and what was wrong; they knew it was wrong for Sunday school children to have been bombed in Birmingham, wrong for black children to have been denied equal access to education in Topeka, wrong for their own state capitol to have been built in part by slaves.

But the question they had to ask themselves was whether or not they were prepared to bear the cost of justice when it would so profoundly affect their own lives.

"We enjoyed privileges we treated as rights," Mullin said, "and it was not easy to contemplate giving up those privileges. Nor was it easy to confront the notion that beliefs we had long held were, in fact, indefensible. Change is painful that way."

Mullin tells a story of one man who in many ways epitomized what his church went through as they struggled with the question of how they may have been contributors to the racial injustices of their own city. "A man I will call Frank, one of the leaders of the church, phoned and asked to see me the next morning in my study. Frank was fiercely conservative, had been his whole life, was an unapologetic segregationist, and had no use whatsoever for Dr. King or the principles he espoused. I knew I was in for an earful.

"He didn't disappoint. He came in, sat across the desk from me, and with fire in his eyes and anger in his belly, told me, 'Joe, I disagree with *everything* you people stand for! I truly do!' But then an interesting thing happened. He paused, sat back for a minute, sagged, stoop-shouldered, and actually began to weep. And with his face in his hands he said quietly, 'But I know in my heart you're right.' "5

This was Frank's crossroads, the point at which the weight of confession met the temptation of denial. It is the place we all come to, whether collectively or individually, where we must choose between a faith that bends itself to our will or a will that bends itself to our faith. And in choosing we decide whether ours is the Christ who dwells only in idyllic places where faith comes easy or the one who also summons us to make difficult and sometimes dangerous choices.

It is not a decision we make once in our life, not a threshold we cross without looking back. Rather, it is the question implied every day, in every moral challenge we face. Whether it's cheating on our bowling score or on our spouse, countenancing intolerance with silence, or valuing popularity or property above kindness, when we *satisfy a want at the expense of an ought,* we follow the example of the disciple who three times in the dead of night let his timidity get the better of his integrity. We take the path of easy ignorance. Like the royalty of old who traveled in shuttered buggies so that they would not have to look at the human deprivation on which their own wealth relied, we shield ourselves from those realities most likely to disrupt our day or disturb our slumber. For, as Anaïs Nin observed, "life shrinks or expands according to one's courage."6

On the other hand, there are times when boldness gets the better of discretion, when we challenge unjust assumptions and question unfair laws, or defend the rights of the many over the privileges of the few. Or, more pointedly, there are times when we do so even if it means sacrificing our own material comforts or cherished beliefs. It was not without risk or cost that the prohibitionist movement, the suffrage movement, the antiwar movement, the civil rights movement, the children's rights movement, the antiapartheid movement, the sanctuary movement took hold in houses of worship throughout America and elsewhere. And such happenings, past and present, proclaim our faith more heartily than any creed we'll ever recite, any prayer we'll offer, or any hymn we'll ever sing.

This is what Frank did that morning in Mullin's office. It was a moment of conversion for him because, head in hand, he could no longer deny what he knew to be the truth. It was his "Who do *you* say that I am?" moment, when confession was made, and prejudice was laid bare. Stubborn old certainties, around which he once fashioned the very values by which he lived, were rattled to their core. A new being had to be coaxed from the shadows and brought into that morning light, the dawn that followed the crowing of the cock. Like the waters in which he was once baptized, his tears would wash him clean.

I'd like to believe it was a transformative moment for this erstwhile bigot, but in all honesty I don't know what happened next. I don't know whether Frank's moment of insight had the durability to carry him over the long haul or whether, after he left that office, the first sight of a black man or woman would incite suspicion or arouse disdain. Perhaps he indeed did become a new man. Or perhaps, as might have been the case for any of us, his outpouring was like one of those Southern cloudbursts on a spring morning, making for great drama but then passing quickly and leaving little memory of it ever having happened. Some transformations take years to evolve, and some die before even being given the opportunity. It can be a long time before we venture out of that little boat and step upon the stormy seas, and longer still before we do so without the fears and doubts that threaten to pull us under. We cling to the familiar because, although we want *to be changed* we don't necessarily want *to change*; we don't want to change the old for the new. It's too hard, and old habits, like gum on a shoe, aren't easily shed, particularly when we don't yet have faith in the new habits we want to put in their place.

## The Church in All Her Imperfect Glory

What made Peter stay faithful to Jesus' mission after Peter denied him that night? In light of what happened that night, I am left to question how, after Jesus' death, he found it in himself to fulfill his destiny and lead that young church into the first millennium of the new era. Whatever sense of superiority he may have once enjoyed for having been first called, whatever exuberance was stirred by the hope that sprung from that empty tomb, had to have been greatly subdued by the memory of what he had done. He was a compromised man now; but still, by all appearances he went on to fulfill the mandate Jesus bestowed on him. But how? Where did his conviction come from to soldier on in the name of the one he had so utterly failed in his time of greatest need?

The answer may well lie in something Jesus said to Peter in a conversation that in all likelihood took place as late as a few days before their fateful entry into Jerusalem. They had gathered in Capernaum, a large, crowded city on the coast of Galilee, a place they had come to frequently in Jesus' ministry. It was perhaps the last time Jesus would be alone to instruct his disciples, in a setting they had come to be comfortable in, without the crowds encroaching on him or the authorities looking to arrest him.

"Lord," Peter asks, "how often shall my brother sin against me, and I forgive him? As many as seven times?" to which Jesus replies, "I do not say to you seven times, but seventy times seven" (Matt. 18:21–22).

What's poignant here is not that Jesus is saying this but that he is saying it *to Peter*. The question is not hypothetical, nor the answer casual, because Jesus is addressing the very man who, more than anyone, will soon need that forgiveness, the way a gasping man needs a breath of air. Jesus is not telling Peter how many times to forgive his brother; he is telling him that *he* is forgiven, unconditionally, incalculably, infinitely, even for the sins he has not yet committed. It is the forgiveness that theologian Reinhold Niebuhr called "the final form of love."[7]

"Before the cock crows twice, you will deny me three times," Jesus said, to which he might have added, "and let me tell you what else you will do. There will be days when you'll wish I had never chosen you to lead the church in my absence, and days when you'll wish you'd never even met me. Responsibilities will be shirked. You will lose your temper over trivial matters and ignore momentous ones. You'll have cruel thoughts about people you love, crave power that is not yours to have, and envy the languorous lives of the idle rich. And I will forgive you all this.

"But you will also do other things," he might continue. "You will also give what little money you have to a destitute family, even if you have no idea where *your* next meal is coming from. You will open your doors to the fatherless, the friendless, even the faithless. You will listen with patience to sad stories and will do whatever is in your power to soothe the pain of the storytellers. You will sit up long nights by the side of the ill and the dying and never breathe a word about your own weariness, and when death does come, you will weep with the widow, and open your home to her as if it is her own."

As will we. Like Peter, we will both embrace and deny the awesome presence of God in our lives and the response it is meant to compel. On more occasions than we care to acknowledge, we suffer those moments when anger gets the better of patience, doubt the better of hope, and indifference the better of compassion. But so too do we, in a moment of sheer clarity, hear the voice of the angels summoning us to a higher good. It is a voice that can come from anywhere, of course, at any time and in any form. But however it comes to us, be it in an Easter hymn in a worship hall or in a song of protest outside its doors, the words are the same: "But who do *you* say that I am?"

# The Tragedy That Was Judas

*Every act of dishonesty has at least two victims; the one we think of as the victim and the perpetrator.*

—Lesley Conger[1]

*Then one of the twelve, who was called Judas Iscariot, went to the chief priests and said, "What will you give me if I deliver him to you?" And they paid him thirty pieces of silver. And from that moment he sought an opportunity to betray him.*

—Matthew 26:14–16

*F*or all the years the Passion story has been told and retold, has any character been targeted for a greater portion of our scorn than Judas? Whereas for the other followers the death of Jesus meant liberation from their sins, for Judas it meant the captivity of his guilt. Judas did not accuse, try, condemn, sentence, mock, or spit upon him. He did not put a whip to the back of his Lord, nor did he drive the nails or weave the thorns. But those were actions committed by Jesus' avowed enemies. The crime of betrayal could have been committed only by one of his friends, and it is that breach of friendship that makes it so despicable, let alone so indecipherable.

Was his the act of a sane man gone suddenly mad? Probably not, because it was too premeditated, too carefully planned and coordinated with the Roman authorities. Was it really the money that tempted him? Again, not likely; the compensation was so paltry as to be nearly insignificant. And whatever the forces may have been, they were not there at the outset of Jesus' ministry, for why would

Judas suffer the deprivations of discipleship unless he believed in the one who was leading them?

## The Devolution of a Disciple

Surely Judas must have been at first as enthusiastic as any of Jesus' other followers. He wouldn't have been chosen to join them otherwise. Like his fellow disciples in those heady early days, Judas was edified by Jesus' teachings and transformed by his miracles. He was overwhelmed by the adoration of the multitudes who wished only to touch a piece of Jesus' garment and no doubt felt immensely privileged to be so closely associated with Jesus. Hopes were high and things were good.

But somewhere along the line, through some constellation of events and experiences, things started going terribly wrong. Perhaps Judas was unsettled by some of Jesus' preaching and thought himself not strong enough of character to be a faithful follower. Jesus, after all, had taught them that a true disciple will "deny himself and take up his cross," a tall order for anyone. He also told them that discipleship meant forgiving their enemies "seventy times seven," turning the other cheek, and praying "for those who persecute them"—a lot to ask of a people who were encouraged to take an eye for an eye. And perhaps most dauntingly, Jesus told them that true disciples resisted all "defilements of thought," by which he meant that even impure *intentions*, whether acted on or not, were intolerable, though invisible, instances of spiritual weakness. Unless we truly aspire to the same moral purity we can only imagine what kind of discipline (from the word, "disciple") it required on their parts to reject not only destructive behavior but tainted thoughts.

Or perhaps it wasn't the moral demands so much as the hard-

> "It was when faith exploded, when hope was fragrant and when they discovered the scope, the scale, the width and the depth of love they had never suspected."
> —Antony, Russian Orthodox archbishop of England

ship and perils of an itinerant life that eroded Judas' resolve. He may have found that while the others could bear the physical and emotional toll of such an existence, he could not. He may even have resented Jesus for imposing this life upon them, and may have resented himself as well for not being up to it.

And in thinking just a little further about Judas's downfall, let's not be too quick to assume the others were not complicit. The disciples were an uneven bunch, to say the least. When Jesus announced that one of them would betray him, many, if not all, of them responded by saying, "Is it I?" as if knowing that they too were capable of such a deed. In earlier days they were also known to grow impatient at followers who demanded Jesus' time. They made promises they did not keep. They fought over who was first in Jesus' eyes. And if in their jockeying for first place they fell into a kind of hard-edged hierarchy, perhaps Judas fell the farthest. After all, in an age when tribal affiliations meant everything and strangers were viewed with suspicion bordering on contempt, Judas was the only one among the Twelve who was not from Galilee. He was the outsider, and perhaps he was not allowed to forget it.

But whatever the triggers, as Judas became increasingly distanced from the hope and excitement of those early days, he probably felt that outsider status increasing. In his unhappiness he would have felt marginalized from the others, as he no doubt believed that, unlike him, they had complete confidence in their calling. He may have doubted whether he even belonged among them and have come to see himself as something of an impostor, appearing to be a good disciple but in his heart wanting only to escape this harsh way of life and its dangers. He would be filled with these dark secrets that he would have to keep to himself. And if Judas was simply nagged by feelings of reluctance before their final entry into Jerusalem, he was surely overwhelmed by them afterwards.

In those final days the risks intensified and, with them, Judas's alienation from Jesus, his cause, and his other followers. Early in the week, the Jesus who once enjoyed the adulation of great crowds had told the few who were left that he would soon die a lonely, condemned man. To the Twelve, this hesitant little band of men, that meant not only that they would be left to fend for themselves, but that their lives too would be in danger. Such is the risk of allying ourselves with unwelcomed truth. His allegiance to Jesus worn threadbare by demons and disappointments known only to him, Judas no longer saw himself willing to take that risk. For thirty shekels—about the price of a cheap slave—he betrayed the man whose sole desire was to set him free.

## Forgiveness beyond His Grasp

But the story doesn't end here, nor is Judas's betrayal of Christ even its climax. It is what happens next to this tortured, pathetic man that bears the full weight of human tragedy. The misery into which he sinks over his action represents his greatest failure, because in his consuming guilt he cannot see that he is already forgiven.

Consider the timing, the order in which things happened. It is not by accident that immediately after Jesus has accused Judas, he turns and offers the disciples—Judas included—the ceremonial meal we now call the Lord's Supper. What is the meal's purpose but to assure them all that his body is given for them, and that his blood is shed for them, *for the forgiveness of their sins*? He is telling them, "Although your thoughts might burrow into the circles of hell, you can be forgiven. Those same thoughts can claw their way into the light of day to emerge again in word and deed; you can still be forgiven. Betrayal takes many forms, but forgiveness makes no exceptions, for 'the wretchedness of men [*sic*] equals the mercy of God.'" The depth and breadth of the divine promise, the promise that stretches back thousands of years to Abraham and forward infinitely into the future, to generations not yet alive, was to be found that night, in its entirety, in that small crust of bread and that simple cup of wine.

The tragedy is that his message was lost on Judas. His death at his own hand would become the counterpoint to his master's crucifixion: one bore witness to eternal hope and the other to relentless despair.

"I think when Judas fled from his hanged and fallen body, he fled to the tender help of Jesus, and found it—I say not how. He was in a more hopeful condition now than during any moment of his past life, for he had never repented before. But I believe Jesus loved Judas even when he was kissing him with a traitor's kiss; and I believe he was his savior still."

—George Macdonald

## Unlearning Behavior

I do not believe this despair *is* unique to Judas. A good many of us have times when—whether we should be offering it or receiving it—we have an ambivalent relationship to forgiveness, primarily because bestowing forgiveness can feel so alien and unnatural to us. The prospect of showing mercy to one who has wronged us contradicts our almost reflexive desire to retaliate for having been wronged.

But it is possible to resist the desire to even the score. Some years ago, New York's then-governor Mario Cuomo was engaged in a debate about capital punishment. He was asked if he—an opponent of the death penalty—would nonetheless wish the death sentence imposed in a hypothetical case in which his own wife was the victim of a brutal murder. "Of course I would!" Cuomo thundered, but then added, "*And that is precisely why I am opposed to the death penalty.* Because a just society must be built on a foundation stronger than one man's desire for revenge!"[2] Cuomo's point was simple enough: even if the most impulsive thing to do is to float with the tide, there are times in our lives when the most noble thing to do is to strain against it.

That desire for revenge that Cuomo referred to is why forgiveness was such a pronounced theme in Jesus' teaching and in the teaching of the psalmists, the prophets, and the patriarchs who came before him. Forgiveness is fundamental to justice, but it requires the *un*learning of deeply ingrained, culturally supported behaviors. It is like trying to untie a tight old knot.

I am reminded of a story I heard from a patient I saw some years ago, a man named Bruce, who was working very hard but with scant results to change some old and destructive patterns of aggressive behavior. Bruce recounted a dream that came to symbolize for him just how hard it was to make the corrections he wanted to make: "I dream I am in a car, on a dirt road. I drive the car to a fork in the road, and I go to the right. I'm never clear as to why I turn that way or what's at the end, but this is what I do. The next thing I know, I am at the beginning of the road again, and do the same thing. I repeat this over and over, until the road is worn so deep with ruts that when the car reaches the fork, I don't have to steer it; it just bends obediently to the right.

"One day, though, I get to the fork, step on the brakes, and wonder what would happen if I went to the left instead. But I can't. The ruts are too deep."

The ruts are too deep. The tide is too strong. The impulse of one angry ex-governor to see another man die for his sins is too compelling to be kept at bay without the help of a body of laws.

But Jesus' death calls us to rise above that impulse and embrace the notion that just as God forgives us, we must forgive one another. To embrace that notion, to hear and to heed it, is to make of us a people who prize mercy above vengeance, pardon above retaliation, compassion above retribution.

Unfortunately, there's no reason to believe that the people of first-century Palestine organized themselves around such lofty principles. So perhaps living in a culture that was reluctant to dispense forgiveness made it difficult for Judas to receive it. Nor have we come all that far in the centuries since. A young mother I once knew typified this struggle in a quarrel she had with her nine-year-old daughter. The previous week the child had carelessly broken a living room lamp.

"How did you handle the situation?" I asked her.

"I was angry, she was crying. It was a mess. She told me she was sorry and I told her, 'Well, sorry doesn't begin to fix the lamp now, does it?'"

No, I thought, an apology doesn't fix the lamp. But it could begin to fix the relationship. That is, of course, if the mother knows what to do with her daughter's overture. In her own timid way the girl was making her confession; she was admitting her mistake and preparing for her fate. But her mother's refusal to accept it meant only that the next time the child did something to stir her anger, the girl might be less forthcoming, more guarded. There would be less room for reconciliation between the two. And from there the pattern would repeat itself, and *their* rut would deepen, making it increasingly difficult for the two of them to ever steer themselves toward reconciliation. Eventually, frustrated by her inability to find the forgiveness she sought, the girl would stop looking for it.

This can happen between a mother and a daughter, but just as easily between a husband and wife. And between sibling rivals and warring nations, erstwhile friends and estranged siblings. The wounds can be deep, the anger pitched, the precipitant forgotten, and the hurt made no less heavy by the passage of time. But none of that will matter, not ultimately, if through courage tinged with grace and freed from ego, entrenched enemies will cede rage to reconciliation and fear to trust.

Forgiveness does not come easily, even with our best efforts. But without our best efforts it may not come at all, for the dance of forgiveness is complicated, and its two partners—perhaps willing, perhaps reluctant or uncertain—must learn to figure it out together. It requires from one the humility to confess contrition, and from the other the generosity to bestow absolution. But lest we think that forgiveness can't be learned, that some ruts are *too* deep to pull ourselves out of, consider the story of one of the most grievous injustices of modern times.

## On Bended Knee

The Truth and Reconciliation Commission of South Africa, led by Archbishop Desmond Tutu, was established in 1995 in order to help that country begin to heal from the wounds inflicted on it by over forty years of apartheid rule. The commissioners were not so naive as to think their work would erase the sins of the past or make adequate recompense for the incalculable damage that had been done. Not all the dead would be remembered, and not all the nightmares would be forgotten. Nor could they return to a woman the years lost in prison for a crime she did not commit, or to her children the inalienable right of being raised by their mother. But what they could do was to give voice to people's sadness and anger. And so they did. They provided a platform for the victims to be heard—in some cases, reminiscent of Psalm 23, in the presence of their enemies, the ones responsible for inflicting their pain. They also gave the guilty an opportunity to confess their crimes and repent their ways. People were held accountable, and penalties—harsh, but not vindictive—were meted out. Restitution, not retribution, was their motivating force; so the aim of the proceedings was not to punish for punishment's sake but to lay the foundation for a society in which persons—some of whom had suffered mightily at the hand of other South Africans—could live as one nation.

> "Evil is the stone on which the good sharpens itself."
> —Dorothy Green

"They tried to take *our* humanity away," the archbishop told me shortly before the commission was formally constituted, "but in the very process, by their very behavior they stripped themselves of *their* humanity. The task of the commission must be to restore *all* of our humanity."[3] The extent to which it has succeeded will be determined years from now, but one thing is certain: had South Africa *not* demonstrated this kind of rare moral strength, its future would certainly have been written by the sins of its past.

My admiration for people who confess their sins and forgive others theirs runs so deep because neither confession nor forgiveness has ever come easily to me. When I feel wronged, my anger rises reflexively and patience comes too late—if at all. I appreciate a perverse power I hold over someone who has assumed the role of the supplicant, petitioning for my forgiveness. I have something he wants, and in my anger I may not be disposed to giving it to him unless he squirms a little for it. When this happens, mercy becomes the hostage we're not eager to release without ransom, because doing so means giving up our claim to that power. We want something in return. All of this I see in others in their lesser moments, but I also see it writ large in myself, and it does not make me proud.

When in those situations I finally *do* relent and offer forgiveness I'd like to say I do so as a gesture of magnanimity—but my hunch is that often it's simply driven by a routine that has gone stale. Like a kid ditching an old toy, I forgive the other because *I* have tired of the breach between us, and it's now in my interest that we be made whole again. And the real tragedy, of course, is that ending the standoff by simply calling it a day does not make us whole. It douses a few flames but the embers will smolder for a long, long time.

Perhaps this is why it can feel so difficult to receive forgiveness: we are afraid that by putting ourselves in the position of the vulnerable one we will be abused by the other's power. I don't know which situation is logically prior to the other, and it probably doesn't really matter. What does matter is that we not make the same mistake—over and over again—that Judas made, warping the crucifixion into an act of bondage rather than liberation. What matters is that we do not betray the spirit of the divine gesture, that we accept its premise and its promise, that we rise above our most human of impulses, that we shed grudges instead of bearing them, respond with love rather than react with rage, confess our sins rather than profess our blamelessness, and find in the death of Christ the ultimate expression of a love we can neither earn nor repay.

# Pilate, Herod, and the Myth of Leadership

*One has to be a lowbrow, a bit of a murderer, to be a politician, ready and willing to see people sacrificed, slaughtered, for the sake of an idea, whether a good one or a bad one.*

—Henry Miller[1]

*And Herod with his soldiers treated him with contempt and mocked him; then, arraying him in gorgeous apparel, he sent him back to Pilate.*

—Luke 23:11

*So when Pilate saw that he was gaining nothing, but rather that a riot was beginning, he took water and washed his hands before the crowd, saying, "I am innocent of this man's blood; see to it yourselves."*

—Matthew 27:24

*A* large and august church has called a new senior minister to their pulpit to be their spiritual leader. With expectations running high on his inaugural Sunday, the minister, appreciating the gravity of the moment, has gone out and purchased an elegant preacher's robe that is no less baroque than his new surroundings. He is looking quite stylish, he thinks to himself.

At the proper time in the service the preacher ascends to the pulpit to deliver the longest, most rambling, most obscure, and generally most forgettable sermon the congregation has ever heard, leaving most of them feeling somewhere between indignant and incredulous about their role in calling him to this position.

After the service, he rushes up to the head of the search committee responsible for hiring him, one of those quiet sorts of people who, when they do speak, do so in understatements that are sure to be taken quite seriously. "So, what did you think of my sermon?" the preacher eagerly asks.

The man rubs his chin, looks at the ground, thinks for a moment, and says, "Well, it's a nice robe."

As an old political activist once told me apropos of the governance of our city, "there is leadership, and there is the appearance of leadership." Or, as Saul Alinsky, the community organizer, aptly noted, "the only way to *be* a leader is to *have* a following."[2]

Both Pilate and Herod were in positions of leadership, but neither was a leader. Pilate, a lifelong government bureaucrat, was the governor appointed by Rome to oversee this relatively insignificant occupied territory. Herod, in contrast, inherited his position; he was a "king." But his rule extended over just a small portion of what had been his father's domain, and because of the presence of Rome his responsibilities were severely restricted.

Still, they shared certain attributes. Each man had power at his disposal but masked his failure to lead by taking advantage of that power only to satisfy his own desires. And the only way either man could convince himself that he had a following was by interpreting fear as respect, because what little credibility they held among their shared constituency was not the kind a statesman earns from a record of service but the kind a despot extorts from the tip of a sword.

Pilate was a coward, Herod a brute. Pilate wanted only to keep his job, Herod to aggrandize himself by building great buildings. Pilate was an outsider regarded with suspicion; Herod an insider regarded with disdain. Neither paid much heed to the needs of the people they governed. And when it came to the crisis presented by the arrest of Jesus, each was afraid of the reaction it would generate among the people they were incapable of leading, and wanted Jesus' fate sealed in the other's court.

It is sad that we can only speculate as to how history might have been written, had either the Roman prefect or the Judean king been a statesman who valued justice over expediency. Sadder still is the fact that in the centuries since, each man has remained as much an example as an anomaly of the ways of government. Were we to eliminate from the rolls of history all the kings and emperors, the queens and czars, presidents and prime ministers and dictators for life who have ruled by intimidation, prospered by dint of corruption, or legislated by a morality of equivocation, the names on those rolls would be scant indeed.

> "Idealism is the noble toga that political gentlemen drape over their will to power."
> —Aldous Huxley[3]

## A Governor Contemptuous of Those He Was Called to Govern

That Pilate cared little about the religious sensitivities of the Jews he governed was evidenced in his tenure as prefect, as recorded by the ancient historians Philo and Josephus. On one occasion, in an act of provocation designed to remind the Jews that Rome was in charge of Jerusalem, he intentionally allowed Roman troops to enter the city and approach the temple compound bearing the flag of the emperor (to the Jews, this was blasphemy, a pagan symbol desecrating their holiest shrine), and on another he hung gold shields inscribed with the names of pagan deities in his palace at Mount Zion. In both instances the people rose in revolt. The first revolt resulted in Pilate's begrudging capitulation for fear that it threatened his reign; the second ended in the people's appeal directly to the emperor, who ordered that the offending icons be removed. In neither case did Pilate inflict any material harm, which makes me wonder if he failed to see the arrogance of his actions. The damage he wrought was psychological, not material; he humiliated the Jews by disregarding their God and their customs. This kind of behavior has often been a failure of the powerful who impose their will on another country, even those invaders who fancy themselves liberators: They enter the land of the captive, bringing with them their own cultural chauvinism, and then are surprised when they are received not as saviors but as occupiers. They expect celebrations and gratitude; what they find is not rose petals covering the streets but land mines hidden beneath them.

In a third instance of provocation Pilate did inflict material harm, when he looted the temple treasury to pay for a public works project. This time, when the Jews again rioted, he ordered soldiers to dress as civilians, mingle among them, and beat them with staves. Eventually, years after Jesus' death, Pilate became so crass and ineffectual that he was returned to Rome to answer charges of incompetence and was subsequently stripped of his office and his title.

On top of this picture of an insensitive traitor, the Gospels show him to be a weak-willed governor who does everything in his power to avoid having to adjudicate Jesus' case: first he declares him innocent; then he offers to pardon him; after that he offers to flog him, next to turn him over to Herod; finally, cornered and out of options, he allows his execution to go forth but only after first washing his hands of responsibility. But wishing doesn't make it so, and Pilate cannot absolve himself of responsibility in the state-sponsored killing of an innocent man when he himself is the head of the state. Denying responsibility for something you have the power to stop is the refuge of cowards. Anytime a person in authority signs an order of execution or a declaration of war, a cut in welfare or a tax break for the rich, his or her signature is a fingerprint of the ethos of his or her rule, and it is unique to its source. And whatever the consequences—success or failure—that governor must be held accountable, both by the people and by history. And this is why, in the end, Pilate's claim of innocence just won't wash.

## The Powerless King

It's always more painful when crimes against a family are committed by one of its own. So even though Herod's offenses were in some ways no worse than Pilate's, his being a Jew made them more reprehensible. We have little historical information about Herod's performance and behavior as tetrarch (loosely defined as "petty ruler"), but even that small amount is illuminating. The son of a father who instituted the slaughter of the innocents because of one newborn baby who courtiers predicted would grow to be a challenge to his authority, Herod is proof positive that the apple, even a rotten one, does not fall far from its tree. If he was fated to be a bad king (and I don't believe anyone's behavior is fated), then he may at least have been predisposed to it by the example set by the father.

Herod pawned himself off as a good and faithful Jew, but in an egregious break with Levitical law that anticipated Henry VIII of England, he divorced his own wife to marry his brother's; when John the Baptist (whom Herod already feared because of the loyalty of the Baptist's followers) took issue with it, Herod used his objection as an excuse to behead him. Known for spying on other local rulers in order to ingratiate himself with Rome, he also commissioned a new capital city, of Roman design, and had the audacity to name it Tiberius (in honor of the reigning emperor). Because the emperor was believed by Romans to be godlike, the Jews took this homage to Tiberius as an offense to their own God. And worse, again in violation of holy law and to the outrage of the citizenry, he built the city atop an ancient, sacred burial ground. Later in his reign, while refortifying the city of Betharamphtha, just east of the Jordan River, he did something similar, renaming that city Livias, this time in honor of the emperor's wife.

Herod's encounter with Jesus is an exquisite metaphor for the irony of a religious fraud condemning a faithful man, a guilty man accusing an innocent. His first thought when he begins to hear rumblings about Jesus' exploits is that Jesus is John the Baptist come back to life. He is haunted, as a guilty man is haunted by his conscience, by the contrast between his own venality and his antagonist's valor. He abuses the laws; Jesus interprets them. He is as despised as Jesus is beloved. He is as much a hedonist as Jesus is materially ascetic, and hungers for power as much as Jesus hungers to empower others. He is a follower of the Roman aristocracy, Jesus a leader of the common masses. He hates this Jesus, who never sullies himself with hatred; he hates him in part because he fears him, and in part because he envies him. Whereas Herod wields the

authority of divine power, Jesus wields the power of divine authority, and just as the pen is mightier than the sword, so too is the
integrity of the prophet mightier than the affectations of the king.

When in Herod's chambers they finally meet, his anger can only
have deepened, because it is here, in Herod's very home, face to
face, that Jesus does what few would ever do, even behind his
back. Jesus goes beyond defying Herod; he ignores him. Jesus,
whose reputation has been built on—among other things—his
golden tongue, the man who is willing to debate the Pharisees on
points of law and the Sadducees on points of custom, who answers
the questions—however contemptuous—posed by Annas and
Caiaphas, and who even rejoins Pilate's vacuous queries, stands
stone silent before Herod. In the face of the indignity, Herod
behaves like the child whose tantrum goes ignored by his parents
and who finally realizes that he cannot manipulate someone
stronger and wiser than he: he gives up.

Rebuked and offended, he orders Jesus clad in a white robe—
the "gorgeous apparel" from Luke (23:11)—and sent back to
Pilate. His actions are significant for two reasons. First, the robe
is a king's robe, Herod's way of implying that Jesus, who
remained silent, claimed before Herod that he himself was king
of the Jews and is therefore guilty of sedition. Second, by sending him back to Pilate for sentencing, Herod, like Pilate, is
attempting to distance himself from the verdict to which he has
given his tacit blessing.

This tinhorn descendant of true kings who commanded armies
and fought in wars cannot break the will of one gentle man who
bears neither weapons nor anger toward his enemies. The one who
teaches forgiveness and second chances, who beseeches his followers to deplore not only violence but violent thoughts, is too formidable an opponent for Herod. Like the fox Jesus accused him of
being (Luke 13:32), Herod cannot face him straight up and impose
an unpopular sentence; he has to resort instead to cunning to bring
this enemy down. In the end, for all the bravado and empty blus-
ter, all his false pride and blind conceit, this make-believe king
stands up from his throne, meets his prisoner eye to eye, and
blinks.

## The Character of the Christ

In some ways we must be grateful to both Herod and Pilate because in their stories we are afforded the richest picture of Jesus' true nature. It is in these brief episodes, more than any others in the Gospels, that Word becomes flesh. When Jesus comes before them, they hold all the cards; he is on their turf, in their custody, and his fate is in their hands. But Jesus knows his enemies perhaps more than they know themselves and uses his own strength of will to exploit their weakness of character.

When Pilate asks Jesus if he is King of the Jews and Jesus answers, "You have said so" (Matt. 27:11), he is putting on Pilate a responsibility that he knows Pilate is loathe to accept, a responsibility he will soon want to wash his hands of. Then, when Pilate tries to avoid the inevitable by telling Jesus it was not he but his accusers who are to blame for his being there ("See how many charges *they* bring against you" [Mark 15:4]), Jesus refuses to answer him. He is, in fact, defying Pilate, telling him with his silence either to set him free and risk the enmity of the mob or to find him guilty and risk sending an innocent man to his death. Pilate, holding forth in the regal robes of his exalted office, ensconced in a palace that represents his imperial power and masks his moral impotence, can do nothing, so he sends him off to his partner in crime, Herod.

Herod does no better, however, his taunts not dignified with so much as a wisp of protest from the condemned man. In his stoic calm Jesus refuses to show fear before Herod, for whom the ability to arouse fear is fundamental to his sense of his own power. Unable to instill dread, Herod is not Herod, and the chimera that is his kingship is laid bare to us. And in the end, the robe that is thrust upon Jesus as he goes from one tormenter to another, the one that mocks him as king, is oddly fitting, for of the three men he alone shows the courage any of us expect from a king.

These stories are in many ways Jesus' last witness to us and perhaps his most important, because in some small way they are the enactment of so much of what he has preached. In the encounters with these two charlatans he exhibits patience and peace, dignity and nonviolence, love of enemy, the courage of conviction, and a sense of hope that transcends even the most hopeless of circumstances. He is telling us to be strong when power is aligned against us and not to allow ourselves to be intimidated when that power tries to bend our wills to its ways. He is also telling us not to stoop to the violence that is the stock in trade of despots. He is reminding us that although the power of faith does not make all situations acceptable, it can make them endurable. And he is preparing us for the inevitable darkness

---

A grassroots community organization in Baltimore called BUILD took issue with a local bank it accused of redlining, or denying mortgages to people who lived in neighborhoods populated largely by people of color. When the group's leadership was, on numerous occasions, denied a meeting with the bank's president, they decided to take matters into their own hands.

On a Friday afternoon (the busiest time of the week in any bank) a number of BUILD members went to the bank and stood on tellers' lines. As their turns came to be served, one would come to the window with thousands of pennies, wishing to deposit them in her account. Then she might spill the pennies and take time picking them up. Someone else would reach the window and speak Spanish to a teller who understood only English. A third activist would come to the window with piles of old statements and begin asking arcane questions about them. When they were finished, they would get back on line again. In short order, the bank was in a state of absolute chaos, with lines stretching out the door and customers in near revolt.

When the president finally came onto the floor to see what was going on, the leadership explained that this was an action of last resort; because he wouldn't agree to meet with them, they had to find a way to get his attention.

It worked. An initial meeting was held on the spot. Subsequent meetings followed. The bank reviewed its mortgage practices. And it corrected them.

---

before the irresistible dawn, the hell that comes when hatred breeds inhumanity beyond our deepest imaginings, and the heaven that ensues when love finally prevails. He is telling us that true nobility can be draped in rags as easily as it is bedecked in robes, for the goodness of a person endows that person with greater stature than any riches, any garment, any crown, any pretense to earthly thrones.

## The More Things Change . . .

These counterfeit kings are no strangers to us. They can be found wherever the power to serve the broadest of our needs is used instead to satisfy the narrowest of their desires.

How is Pilate's foisting Roman paganism on ancient Judea any different from the American usurpation of Navajo burial grounds? How is his washing his hands of the blood of my Lord not a parallel to a president's unwillingness to accept responsibility for sending soldiers and civilians to their deaths in a war that his administration failed to avoid?

And who is the modern-day Herod if not the likes of Nicolae Ceausescu, the Romanian strongman who, at the height of his reign, turned Bucharest into an architectural monument to himself while his people went without food and their schools went without books. And if not in Ceausescu, we surely find Herod mirrored in any so-called leader who has ever dispatched with his enemies by disposing of them: the CEO who drives his competition into bankruptcy through unfair trade practices, the candidate who buys the election, the politician who smears his opponents with lies and innuendo, the head of state who orders assassination by proxy and displays his dismay when the six o'clock news rolls its cameras.

Herod and Pilate are long gone, both victims of their own hubris, both ending their lives in the humiliation of exile. But as long as men and women abuse the power of their office to the detriment of those who put them there, they will never be far from us. This is why the example Jesus set those days in their courts must never be far from us either.

Mahatma Gandhi was beaten with sticks, but he would not rise to the bait of his adversary. Martin Luther King was spat upon, but he would not stoop to the gutter tactics of his oppressor. Nelson Mandela organized a work strike by ANC prisoners on Robben Island until their captors agreed to meet basic human needs to the political prisoners and to treat them with a measure of respect. Betty Williams, a housewife and mother living in Northern Ireland, refused to abide the violence any longer and literally went door to door asking people to come out into the streets and demand peace. For her efforts militants issued death threats against her, and the Nobel committee issued her their 1976 prize for peace. None of these people wore the flowing robes of high office, the robes that are supposed to signify leadership. But each one was a leader—because people followed them, to the shores of the Ganges, the streets of Birmingham, the slums of Soweto, the streets of Belfast. To certain struggle and uncertain fate, people followed—as people will, when given the choice between the Pilate of our revulsions, the Herod of our fears, and the Christ of our hopes. As the great essayist George Sand put it, "they were born kings of the earth far more truly than those who possess it only from having bought it."[4]

# The Mob Calls for Jesus' Crucifixion

*There is little place in the political scheme of things for an independent, creative personality, for a fighter. Anyone who takes that role must pay a price.*
— Shirley Chisholm[1]

*And Pilate again said to them, "Then what shall I do with the man whom you call the King of the Jews?" And they cried out again, "Crucify him." And Pilate said to them, "Why, what evil has he done?" But they shouted all the more, "Crucify him."*
— Mark 15:12–14

*S*ome years ago I was in a packed subway car traveling beneath the streets of Boston to an afternoon appointment. I didn't necessarily have much in common with the people who were there with me. We were just a crowd of strangers. But then something happened: the train stopped between stations and sat there for a while. Now we *did* have something in common, because we were all stuck, stranded, and had someplace else we preferred to be. We'd become a group, that is, a collection of people who share at least one significant trait. And when the train sat there for an inordinately long period of time and the lights went out, frustrations built, temperature rose, tempers shortened, and anger flared at the conductor, who had no answers for us. We were on the verge of becoming a mob, which is also a group, but a group that is overrun with emotion and about to behave in ways none of the individuals might behave under cooler circumstances. Just then the train jerked, the lights flickered on, and off we went. We were strangers again.

When I think of the crowd who gathered outside Pilate's head-quarters, I think of them as a group that became a mob. They started out sharing a certain set of common traits that bound them to one another, for they had a history as Israelites and a heritage as Jews. And if we're going to understand why that group of people became a mob that called for Jesus to die—and let's keep in mind that not everyone in Jerusalem was gathered there—we first have to understand what it was they were a part of.

These people were members of a discrete culture; they lived cheek by jowl in an overpopulated city, practiced the same customs, sang the same music, and ate the same kinds of food. They saw themselves as descendants of Abraham, worshiped the same God he had worshiped, and chafed under an occupation that they believed to be the consequence of their disobedience to that God. There were of course, as there are in any culture, distinctions among them—differences in wealth, taste, values, religious leanings, and so forth. But those differences notwithstanding, these people had a shared identity that was profoundly influenced by the fact that they were, for all intents and purposes, exiles in their own homeland. They were children of Yahweh, and they were living under Caesar's thumb. As is the case with the strangers on the subway, in moments of crisis, surface differences are often overridden by a shared sense of threat that that crisis poses. And this was just such a moment.

Some of those calling for Jesus' death truly believed he was a heretic, while others simply doubted the credibility of what he taught. Still others knew very little about him but had heard rumors of his penchant for stirring up trouble, and this deeply unsettled them. The truth is, some of them may have even strewn palms at his feet not five days earlier. But collectively they sensed a threat, if not to the purity of a faith that may or may not have mattered to them, then at least to their overall well-being under the governance of a Roman procurator who did not gladly tolerate unrest. Simply put, of those who came to insist upon Jesus' guilt, some did so to appease the God of Abraham and others the god of Pilate.

I don't know how many of those people felt such intense venom toward Jesus that they truly wanted him killed, but I do believe that most of them were anxious about what might happen to them should he be kept alive. These were people who lived with the great uncertainties that any oppressed people lived with—taxes could be arbitrarily levied, worship practices compromised, personal freedoms curtailed, homes taken away, all at the behest of the emperor—and as such came to understand that a more obedient society is a more tranquil one, a more tranquil one a less threatening one, a less threatening one a less threatened one. So it was that even though Pilate offered to free Jesus, the mob knew his freedom wouldn't relieve their fears, because Pilate was looking less to spare Jesus his life than to put the responsibility for his death in the hands of his fellow Jews. Pilate was the ultimate oxymoron: a ruthless coward.

But if those people in Jerusalem were not of one mind, why did they seem to speak with one voice? How did their ambivalences get lost in all the noise? Why would some people join in a chant for the death of a man they didn't even know, if all they wanted was the assurance that he posed no threat to their safety and security? The answer, I think, has less to do with the mind of the individual than with the mentality of the group that becomes the mob, because in human affairs, individuality defers to the will of the whole.

## Why Do Groups Form? Why Do We Gather?

Since Adam first got together with Eve, we have recognized the need to gather ourselves—into families, tribes, guilds, classrooms, communities, nations—because together we achieve things we can't achieve alone. The myth of the rugged individualist notwithstanding, we need to work things out together. While doing that, we are conscripted into some groups and voluntarily join others, and we do so because we have a common sense of purpose, principle, value, or task.

And so it was with the people on Pilate's porch; they had many

differences among them, but together they held a shared belief that
Jesus represented some kind of threat to their status quo. If not all
of them wanted him to die, certainly all of them wanted that threat
to die away. But the mood within the group—angry to the point of
being near riotous as it gathered in haste in the heat of the
moment—left little room for discussion or dispute. It spoke with
one voice even if it represented several. It became a mob.

I believe this happened to these people because it happens often.
To begin with, it is the nature of so many groups that when we
choose to be a part of a larger entity, we surrender something of our
personal identity to it. To say that I am an American, or a Christian,
or a Rotarian, isn't to say that I stand foursquare with every value
those groups represent, but rather that, absent debate about those
values, I am, by identifying myself this way, allowing myself to be
defined by my affiliations and allegiances. Our core principles are
intact, but like the grains of sand on the ocean floor, each subtly different from the next, we become indistinguishable from the whole
of which we are a part. This, I believe, is why this passage reads as
if everyone wanted Jesus executed. The crucifixion represented the
lowest common denominator of solutions, the one solution that
would assuage everyone's fears, and as the shouts went up—maybe
from many, maybe from only a few, we'll never know—those in
that mix who would have been satisfied with a less severe solution
had little choice but to endorse what others called for.

On top of this, even those who did call for the cross could do so
in part because they did not have to absorb full responsibility for
their actions. As the theologian Reinhold Niebuhr pointed out, a
group is an inherently more arrogant, self-centered, and ruthless
entity than any of its component parts, and a mob only more so;
either will do things that none of the individuals who comprise it
would do on their own.[2] The morality of a group is far more fluid,
more flexible, and more lenient than that of its members. The reason for this, I think, is that personal guilt can be a powerful motivation to do the good thing and avoid the bad, but when we are
gathered together in the execution of something about which we
are personally ambivalent on ethical grounds, guilt is so thoroughly diffused that it loses its potency.

Blame, we believe, cannot be laid directly at our doorstep; we, at best, grudgingly accept some small shred of it but also convince ourselves that the bulk belongs elsewhere. We do not fully accept the consequences of our actions because it is not us enacting them; it is the sum of the whole. So though these men and women—every one of them—were responsible for inciting Jesus' death, they did not *feel* responsible. They did not call for his death; the mob did.

When evening came, many of those people returned home, played with their kids, ate their supper, and had a good night's sleep, for individually they had done nothing wrong, nothing of great consequence, nothing to be held accountable for.

When one person kills another, he or she is committing a murder, but when a mob calls upon the authorities to do their killing for them, they are keeping the peace. Augustine tells the story in *City of God* of a young pirate who has been captured by the forces of Alexander the Great and comes before the king. He writes: "The king asking him how he durst molest the seas so, he replied with a free spirit, 'How darest thou molest the whole world? But because I do it with a little ship I am only called a thief; thou doing it with a great navy art called a conqueror.' "[3]

## The Group Is Self-Protective

The groups we create and join are often neither inherently good nor inherently bad but lend themselves to things both good and ill. For example, a nation such as ours, with about 300 million people, can't function without some form of government, and when that government uses its power to empower our poor, it is lending itself to the good. But that same government, when it uses that same power to subvert the rights of people, lends itself just as easily to the bad. Sanctity is not just bestowed but earned; the Christian church has had its share of valiant successes and craven failures, having been the initiator of both the Underground Railroad and the Inquisition. And in the Middle East of the twenty-first century, years after the bloodshed of Christ, the bloodshed of Israelis and Palestinians has led in one camp to the construction of a wall and

in the other to the formation of Hamas, an organization that spon-
sors daycare centers, medical clinics, food pantries, and suicide
bombers. Short of living the life of the hermit, we all have little
choice but to be members of any number of groups, some of which
we will have heated quarrels with. Our challenge in those circumstances is to find in our hearts a certain courage that was lacking
that day before Pilate: the courage to dissent. But courage is not an
easy thing to draw upon, because so many groups are—as was that
group—by nature resistant to dissent. And so our temptation is to
remain quiet.

Whether an organized group or an unruly mob, gatherings of
people have discrete identities; they have characteristics that dis-
tinguish them from their "competition." They protect those identities, for even though many groups have mechanisms for change,
their natural inclination is to seek stasis. The Boy Scouts teach love
of family, love of land, and love of country. They also exclude
girls, atheists, and homosexuals from their ranks. So if you're a kid
of liberal proclivities who really wants the Scouts to teach you how
to tie a hitch knot or build a campfire, you have to decide either to
swallow your principles or fight for them, all the while keeping in
mind how slowly the wheels of change do creak and how quickly
retribution can be visited upon the dissident.

In higher-stakes games, in higher-risk neighborhoods, I've
known kids as young as eight years old who join a violent, sometimes murderous street gang, not because they're enamored of the
life, but because they see it as a way to survive and a place to belong.
As one young boy, a bright-eyed but profoundly sad thirteen-year-
old named Jerome, put it to me: "Look, here's the deal. Everyone
else's failed us. Our parents don't care, our teachers don't teach, and
no one's hiring. The preacher tells us to pray and everything's gonna
be alright, but that ain't happening. The cops tell us to keep movin'
or they'll run us in. An' the guys on the street tell us if we don't join
one of the gangs we're gonna get popped.

"I'm not crazy about it. But at least these guys [in the gang], we
care about one another. We got each other's back. We're family. I
feel like I belong."[4] For Jerome, gang life was a Faustian bargain;
by his own admission he truly hated the risks, the drugs, and the

violence, and I think he was too smart to think it was going to lead
to anything good. But he signed on for two reasons: because the
gang would give him an identity and with it a sense of value, of
belonging, and because he had few if any other options. When all
was said and done, Jerome was recruited into a violent group that
would never be anything other than what it was, never bend to suit
his wishes or will. If on principle Jerome decried the drugs and violence that went with this life, he also knew he needed an anchor,
and the gang provided one.

To me Jerome's story is an instructive tragedy, because it paints
so clear a picture of the determination a group can have to define
and protect its collective identity, its sense of self. And it underscores the ambivalence with which we align ourselves with some
of those groups, for even if none of us is destined to live a life as
desperate as Jerome's, he reminds me that in our own small ways
we all insinuate ourselves into groups that don't always reflect
what we think, feel, or believe without some measure of distortion.
I think of Roman Catholics I know who advocate equal rights for
women in the church, and attorneys who have grave doubts about
the impartiality of our justice system and are not afraid to say so.
I think of soldiers who, out of uniform, would never raise a hand,
let alone a weapon, in anger at another human being. I also think
of some of the laborers I knew when I was living in a small New
England city where the only steady employment they could find
was at the local gun-manufacturing plant. The majority of them
weren't paid well enough to climb their way out of poverty, and I
remember how much it pained them to make their living manu-
facturing the very weapons that contributed to the instability of
their own neighborhoods.

To live in a culture is to be a part of many, many subcultures,
which means we are called upon to make many, many compromises. Some of us join street gangs that engage in bloodshed; we
do so because those gangs also practice their own strange form of
brotherhood or sisterhood for kids who are so desperate to be cared
about by *somebody*. Some of us join worshiping communities that
deny equal rights to women, but we do so because those communities have done so much to feed our souls, and may even provide

us an occasional forum to vent our complaints. Some of us assemble the guns that will find their way into our neighborhoods, and we do so because it is the only way to feed our families.

And some of us quietly acquiesce to the violent death of a man of peace because it is easier to silence him than to bear the repercussions that would ensue, should he be allowed to live and be heard.

## The Loneliness of Dissent

So what does it mean to be a member of the loyal opposition? To paraphrase the Synoptic evangelist, the prophet is without honor in his or her own home, which certainly doesn't suggest an easy go of it. Imagine one lone man in that mob before Pilate. He is, say, a blacksmith, a man of modest means and little education, who has a family to look after and debts to pay.

He has been told by some that Jesus is a savior and by others that he is an apostate, a threat to the uneasy peace that exists between the Jews and the Romans. He has heard Jesus speak and finds something unsettling but compelling about the way he interprets the Law and the Prophets. It is different, bold, and imaginative. It breathes life into texts that over the years have become tired and predictable. But his teaching is also contrary to the prevailing wisdom of many of our blacksmith's more literate neighbors, and he is afraid of the uncertainty of what will happen, should Jesus be allowed to continue his ministry. Will there really be riots in Jerusalem? And if so, will the authorities crack down? Will people be able to get to market to buy his products? Will he be able to service his debt? Might he lose his home? And might the critics be right? Might this Nazarene preacher indeed be a fraud, as so many messianic pretenders had been?

The blacksmith has never called for the death of another human being, but he has also never felt so anxious about his future and the future of his family. His friends—some of them more firebrand than he—are going with the others to see the governor and ask that he come along with them. This is why he is there. As the events unfold and he hears the call for Jesus to die, he feels sad but powerless: sad because it has come to this, and powerless because if he tries to appeal for moderation, his words will go unheeded if not unheard. It is not an occasion to sound a contrarian voice, he thinks, it can only invite the enmity and suspicion of others. And so he says nothing. When he goes home and his wife asks him what happened, he distances himself from this event that he has played a part in, and he tells her, "*They* called for his crucifixion."

A group doesn't easily welcome dissent—and a mob doesn't welcome it at all—because dissent threatens its cohesion. The dissident is branded as unfaithful, a traitor, a troublemaker, an instigator, or a deserter of the cause. The price for dissent is the cold shoulder that awaits a cop who breaks his silence on police corruption, the ridicule directed at an adolescent who refuses to take a sip or a smoke at the prom, or the intrusion of privacy that has come with the federal wiretapping of such "anti-American" organizations as the American Friends Service Committee, the American Baptist Church, People for the American Way, and the American Civil Liberties Union. Dissent is an uphill struggle, often made at great price. And it can be as lonely as it is costly.

One of the most chilling threats to the right of Americans to dissent was issued on September 20, 2001, when, in a speech on terrorism before a joint session of Congress, President George W. Bush declared that "he who is not with us is against us," as if blind obedience to the dictates of the executive branch of the U.S. government had become a kind of litmus test of our patriotism. Some weeks later, his press secretary accentuated the president's point when he told the American public that "people had better watch what they say and what they do." I cannot help but be reminded of the words of another statesman, who put it this way: "Ideas are more powerful than guns. We would not let our enemy have guns. Why should we let them have ideas?" It was Joseph Stalin.

Jeanette Rankin was the first woman elected to the U.S. House of Representatives. On December 8, 1941, the day after the Japanese attack on Pearl Harbor, Rankin, a committed pacifist, became the only member of Congress to vote against going to war. Rankin was being faithful to a principle she had espoused years earlier when she defined war as "the slaughter of human beings, temporarily regarded as enemies, on as large a scale as possible."[5] One year later, it cost her her job. Twenty-six years later, she led over five thousand women who called themselves "The Jeanette Rankin Brigade" in a march on the United States Capitol to protest the war in Vietnam.

To the ranks of her lone voice we can also add the likes of Joseph McNeil, a black college student, who on February 1, 1960, joined three fellow students at the lunch counter of a Woolworth's store in Greensboro, North Carolina, asking that the counter be opened to blacks as well as whites. They were refused, and the store closed early to avoid having to serve them. Their gesture was but one pebble of what eventually became a landslide of civilly disobedient sit-ins in the name of civil rights. Five months after their first sit-in, McNeil and his colleagues were served, and Woolworth's declared itself integrated.

But the dissident does not always make a mark in history as Jeanette Rankin and Joseph McNeil did. She may be also the eleven-year-old who befriends the girl no one else will play with, the rabbi who officiates at a divided town's first gay wedding, or the office worker who risks the ire of her boss because she has chosen to honor a picket line outside the building where she works. The dissident is the lone little boy whose temerity born of candor compels him to tell the emperor that he is wearing no clothes.

It is hard to be heard over the voices calling for crucifixions great or small, or choruses that champion sameness for sameness's sake. But there is also comfort to be found in the company of our convictions, in refusing to hide behind mob morality, in being willing to state our beliefs, live our beliefs, and accept the consequences of our beliefs. When it comes to summoning the courage to live out one's faith in this way, I suspect we would be hard pressed to find anyone in that crowd before Pilate so willing. But when I think of the one whose death they called for, I also suspect we would be hard pressed to find anyone *more* willing.

# Simon of Cyrene

*One fire burns out another's burning, One pain is lessen'd
by another's anguish.*

—William Shakespeare[1]

*And when they had mocked him, they stripped him of the
robe, and put his own clothes on him, and led him away to
crucify him. As they were marching out, they came upon a
man of Cyrene, Simon by name; this man they compelled
to carry his cross. And when they came to a place called
Golgotha (which means the place of a skull), they offered
him wine to drink, mingled with gall; but when he tasted
it, he would not drink it.*

—Matthew 27:31–34

Wendell Phillips, the nineteenth-century abolitionist, observed
that opinion is truth filtered through the disposition of the spectator. Unfiltered truth, on the other hand—to the extent that such a
thing is possible—is something we gain not from observation but
from experience.[2] Simon of Cyrene began the day harboring an
opinion and ended it knowing a truth. He had come to Jerusalem
from far away, no doubt simply to partake of a Passover in the Holy
City. But when events unfolded as they did on that early Friday
morning, he was drawn to them. Much the way many of us slow
down at the scene of an automobile accident or a house fire, people lined the streets to look at three condemned men, each bearing
a hundred-pound crosspiece on his shoulders and dragging one
foot behind another to the site of his execution.

We have a dark human curiosity about calamities that are not our own, an odd concurrence of danger and safety. On the one hand, this terrible event could, under other circumstances, just as easily have happened to us or to someone we love, and we are both compelled and excited by the notion that such danger lurks around us. On the other hand, because it *didn't* happen to us, but to someone else, we maintain a certain distance from the event, a filtered truth. We feel the risk, and imagine the pain, but only vicariously and from the protection of a Jerusalem sideline, a police barricade, or the dry side of a fire truck.

One of the men in that procession, beaten and scourged, could no longer walk, and collapsed on the road. The fact that he happened to do so in front of Simon would change Simon from an observer to a reluctant participant, move him from sideline to center stage. And just as our experiences alter our lives—and the more dramatic the experience, the more the dramatic the alteration—this experience may well have changed Simon's life profoundly, for in it he found a truth he did not even come to Jerusalem to look for.

## The Last Mile

There was no one else left to help Jesus now. Not long before their entry into Jerusalem, his disciples had heard him say to them, "If any man would come after me, let him *deny himself and take up his cross* and follow me. For whoever would save his life will lose it, and whoever loses his life for my sake will find it" (Matt. 16:24–25). No doubt they listened to him in rapt attention, nodded their agreement, and looked at each other with the kind of knowing expression that silently says, "Yes, of course, when the time comes, we will do this for him; we will take up the cross." But theirs was the filtered truth of the spectator. By the time that cross was strapped to his back, they had all left. As Matthew records later, shortly after Jesus was arrested, "all the disciples forsook him and fled" (26:56). Each one chose to save his own life, rather than risk losing it for Jesus' sake, and succumbed to what editor George

Appleton called "the cowardice that dare not face new truths."[3] And so the task of bearing the cross fell to a complete stranger.

It is easy to misinterpret the events of this last mile as a kindness either on the part of the Roman soldier, who relieved Jesus of his burden, or of Simon, who bore it. In fact, there was no benevolence on either part.

The soldier, as was custom, needed only to make certain Jesus would still be alive when the cross was lifted at Calvary. As a deterrent to other would-be criminals, the authorities wanted prisoners to suffer the agony—slow asphyxiation—that is peculiar to crucifixion. And because Jesus' body had been so compromised by his beating, this agony was not a sure thing. Weighing the risk, the soldier pointed to Simon and ordered him to help.

That Simon was compelled is important, because it implies he would not have acted of his own accord, and I suspect this is right. To have stepped forward voluntarily would have been the first-century equivalent of stopping at the scene of the car crash or racing into the burning building; it is a rare hero who puts himself or herself in harm's way for the sake of a stranger. What Simon did was not heroic; he had no choice.

But that doesn't mean he wasn't deeply moved by what he did, for in this too he was only human. The filter that separated his opinion from Jesus' reality was—if only faintly and for a short time—lifted, and he saw, no longer obliquely but starkly, what this man was being ordered to endure. When the crosspiece was put on his shoulders, he did not imagine the weight, he felt it. And with it he felt the sweat and blood that had seeped from Jesus' body to warm the wood. He felt the splinters and shards digging into his shoulders. He felt tightness in his arms and his neck as the rigidity of the wood constrained them. He felt his legs buckle and quaver. And perhaps more than any of this, he felt the stares of the spectators, felt both their dark curiosity and their removal from what he and the criminals were now enduring. The vast majority of that crowd was there to witness not a tragedy over which they would later weep, but an event they would recall at dinner that night, and Simon felt this too.

But for him it would become something else entirely. When he reached Calvary and the burden was lifted from his shoulders, he must have been amazed at how unburdened he felt. How grateful he was to be a free man. He was the same man that he was when he awoke that morning. He had no more money and no fewer cares, had not made any new friends or lost any old ones; but something had changed, "as a room has changed," wrote a poet, "when someone new has entered it."[4] The taste of death had given him a deepened appreciation for life, and the weight of the cross that was taken from him had given him a deepened sense of compassion for the one who would now be nailed to it. When in a few moments those crosses were hoisted, Simon saw it all through new eyes, no longer the eyes of a spectator but the eyes of a participant. He tasted the agony of the other, in small dose, and he would not forget it. Like the scrap of bread that is the body broken and the sip of wine that is the blood poured out, it was his communion, his small taste of the larger reality. Not enough to consume or sate him, but enough to know what one human being is enduring for the sake of others.

Simon was the lucky one for having been chosen, not the disciples who fled for their lives. He was lucky because of what he had learned by what he had experienced. What those disciples never fully appreciated was that when Jesus challenged them to take up the cross, he was offering them a gift. Had they stayed, and carried it for him, *they* would have been the ones so much closer to him, so much closer to his pain, and therefore his love. But they chose safety over courage, as most of us would have, as I would have, as Simon would have. And so we would never know. Simon knew, but only because he was forced to know.

## When the Finger Points Not to Simon but to Us

We are defined by many things, including both the burdens we choose and the burdens that choose us. A child is born with severe autism, and the condition changes her family into something they never intended to become; they must make great accommodations in their lives but also in their dreams and expectations, and perhaps even in their theology. A young man—in many ways a boy, really—is conscripted into military service and returns from the battlefield minus a leg or an arm, and he must not only learn new ways of doing things but unlearn old ones, as must those who love him. There's too much rain at planting time, or too little, or a seedling blight gets the better of the crops, and a farm five generations in the same family is lost to foreclosure. The family is left

Many years ago, in the seminal stages of the modern civil rights movement, a group of ministers gathered to fight entrenched discrimination in Montgomery, Alabama. The group was comprised of a veritable who's who of respected black clergy in the Montgomery area, but when they were preparing to launch a bus boycott in protest against the treatment of Rosa Parks, the consensus among its de facto leaders was that, to present their concerns to the wider public, they needed a spokesperson who did *not* carry the baggage that came with the internal politics of such a highly charged group. For this reason they anointed a well-spoken newcomer who had few ties to the community and therefore little baggage, Martin Luther King, Jr., to represent them to the world.

For the rest of his life King would refer to this moment as the one when he first bore his cross, his sense of obligation to serve the cause of racial freedom, in a leadership role that was bestowed on him through no initiative or self-promotion of his own. It was for King a sacred, if uninvited, obligation.

to figure out how to do without something each one of them was born into, and why it is that the prayers they offered up every Sunday at the little prairie church have gone unanswered.

We don't know when the finger will point our way, and when it does, there is no purpose in asking why, because to ask is to assume there is some sort of ethereal logic behind who suffers and who does not. God did not place Simon at that spot at the roadside, any more than he inflicts a child with a congenital disorder, runs a bullet through a soldier's limb, or invites a plague upon a family's livelihood. No, the question we must ask is not why the cross is lashed to our shoulders, but what we will do with it. What will we see that we would not have otherwise seen? What filter will be removed that will allow us to replace an opinion with a truth?

I once had a patient by the name of Stephen, a perceptive and very successful businessman with a wonderful wife and a loving young son. Stephen was experiencing bouts of depression, and at some point our work turned toward his relationship with his own parents and the kind of upbringing he had had.

Stephen's parents were materially generous but emotionally stingy people; they gave him, in his words, "everything I could ever want—except, of course, time and affection." The dynamics that were at work here are not important here; what is important is the revelation Stephen had after parsing much of this out. "I can't change the way I was raised," he told me, "but what I can do is take a good hard look at it and make sure that I don't make those same mistakes with *my* son." And then, after a brief, reflective pause, he added, "I honestly don't know that I would be so aware of the need to show my boy how much I love him—to really *show* it, not expect him to assume it—if it hadn't been absent in my own childhood."

What Stephen was talking about was bearing the cross of an unhappy experience but then using it, perhaps the way Simon did, to see a reality he might otherwise have missed. Just as Simon could gain some small glimpse of the agony of another man,

> An extraordinary scene near the end of Ibsen's *A Doll's House* captures the long-standing pain of a woman who has borne the cross of sexism and the oppression of women, but who throws it off with great relish when her moment of awareness strikes. Torvald, the husband, is upbraiding Nora, his wife, whom for the many years of their marriage he has treated like a second-class citizen.
>
> "First and foremost, you are a wife and a mother!" Torvald storms, to this woman who has always deferred, childlike, to his every word.
>
> "That I don't believe any more," Nora answers, defiant. "I believe that first and foremost I am an individual, just as much as you are."

Stephen could gain a sense of what it would mean to his son to go through his childhood unsure of his parents' love for him. He took something long relegated to his past, dead and gone, and gave it new life to the end that it might bear fruit for the benefit of others.

There is an old Turkish legend that speaks eloquently to this point; it is the story of a third-century martyr by the name of Papas of Lyconia. During the reign of the Roman emperor Maximian, Papas was arrested and condemned for exercising his Christian beliefs. As punishment he was tied to a tree that had for years been barren, never yielding any fruit. As the legend has it, Papas died there, tied to the tree. And the tree began to bear fruit again.

It would be easy for us to ridicule a story like this as fantastic, a fable or an anecdote the likes of which would charm a child. But historical accuracy is no more relevant here than the accuracy of a Homeric saga or a Hasidic tale, because the real point is that life can be extruded from death. Papas's martyrdom was not in vain, the story tells us, because by bearing his cross he became an exemplar of faith and fortitude for others. And that is a lesson that bore fruit well before the time of Papas and will continue to bear fruit long after our own time.

## No One's Cross Need Be Theirs Alone

The empathy Simon felt for Jesus resulted from an experience that was not of his choosing; the cross was foisted on him. But empathy needn't always be acquired this way. We can look for opportunities to help others bear their crosses because no one should have to suffer in isolation. The pain I feel is no different from yours, no different from my closest friend's or my fiercest enemy's, and while to experience pain is necessary, to learn from it is priceless.

If I lose my job or my health, if I am bruised by the thoughtlessness of people I don't know or hurt by the insensitivities of those I do, I am not the first, nor will I be the last, to suffer thus. And it does my soul good to be reminded of this, because it defines suffering as a part of the human condition and beckons me to look with softer eyes on those around me whose lives I might otherwise either not even consider, or consider with little patience for their wounds and woes. Because in the end, we are all connected—like it or not—by the struggles that beset us and the joys that enchant us, and by our moral capacity to see to it that life need not be either

I remember going through our mail one evening and finding that we were one of many families who received a form letter from a neighbor whom we did not know, a man named Michael, asking us to sponsor him in an upcoming AIDS walk. At first glance I didn't give it much thought, but when I read the letter carefully, not cursorily, and came to the sentence that read, almost as an afterthought, "I walk in memory of my daughter, who died of AIDS," a chord was struck deep inside me. Being parents of a daughter, my wife and I were happy to contribute, as were many others. Michael was Simon of Cyrene that day, bearing the cross for all bereaved parents. And in a small way, we too were like Simon, because we took his pain and made it our own, alleviated it, if only for a few dollars and a few steps on his journey.

celebrated or endured alone. This way, when we bear the cross—our own or another's, under duress or of our own volition—we are really bearing it for all the world.

So when we think of Simon, and of the unfiltered truth he saw when he shared Jesus' burden, we can realize that he came to know that burden as few others ever have, with a depth and authenticity that is not the purview of the mere spectator. Perhaps he came to care about Jesus, and about the fate of the others who would be crucified with him, not as criminals or even as victims, but as human beings. And if so, I like to believe that it did not stop there. I like to believe that when the crosspiece was removed from his tired shoulders, he surveyed that mountain, saw the angry mob and the weeping women, the soldiers and the shopkeepers, the hierarchy who had a vested interest in this execution and the onlookers, like himself, there only because they were irresistibly, inexplicably drawn to that razor's edge between danger and safety. He saw them all and somehow felt a kinship to them all. From the executioner who drove the nails into Jesus' hands to the mother who wept at his feet, Simon recognized that in the end none of us is a spectator, really. We all participate in this terrible, hopeful, dreadful, glorious experience that is life. How wonderful it would be if only we would all know this—not with the reserve of the one who stands on the sidelines, but with the passion of the ones who have walked the dusty streets, bearing, as the Sufis say, that portion of the world's pain that has been entrusted to their care.

# The Good Thief

*Friendship needs no words—it is loneliness relieved of the anguish of loneliness.*

—Dag Hammarskjöld

*One of the criminals who were hanged railed at him, saying, "Are you not the Christ? Save yourself and us!" But the other rebuked him, saying, "Do you not fear God, since you are under the same sentence of condemnation? And we indeed justly; for we are receiving the due reward of our deeds; but this man has done nothing wrong." And he said, "Jesus, remember me when you come in your kingly power." And he said to him, "Truly, I say to you, today you will be with me in Paradise."*

—Luke 23:39–43

## To Speak Not of God's Will, but of Our Own

When a pious young German couple asked the renowned theologian Dietrich Bonhoeffer to perform their wedding ceremony, he agreed to do so and, in his sermon for the occasion, offered them one piece of unsolicited advice: "Do not be in too much a hurry to speak here of God's will and guidance," he wrote. "It is obvious, and it should not be ignored, that it is your own very human wills that are at work here. . . . You yourselves, and you alone bear the responsibility for what no one can take from you."[1]

I've long thought that Bonhoeffer saw in these two lovers a dangerous innocence of thought, one in which all things consequential could be attributed to a more activist God than he himself believed in. I think he wanted to remind them that we are in large part the sum total of the decisions we make; while God may inform those decisions, we are accountable for their content and consequence. When we pray, "Thy will be done," Bonhoeffer would argue, we are not surrendering responsibility by attributing our actions to God. Rather, we are hoping that our own power of human discernment is brought to bear such that we are prompted to do the right thing, the faithful thing in the commerce of our daily comings and goings.[2] He would know, having composed this sermon not in a vacuum but in a German prison cell in 1943, as a member of the resistance, having been implicated in a plot to take the life of Adolf Hitler. It would ultimately cost Bonhoeffer his own life, and he did not hold God responsible.

Bonhoeffer's point is that a couple can no more lay on God blame for a bad marriage or credit for a good one than an athlete can thank God for winning the big game, a worker for landing the big job, or a student for passing the big test. Nor can a martyr consider God responsible for an act of personal courage or of failure. *We alone bear the responsibility for what no one can take from us.*

I think of this when I consider the thieves on the cross and the choices they made. We do not know anything more about them than that they were hung aside Jesus in his final hours, but perhaps we can surmise—cautiously—*something* of their lives. The very fact of their anonymity—that we don't learn their names, the nature of their character, or their crimes—leads me to believe that at least in the eyes of the evangelist they were men of little or no importance. Chances are their crimes were petty, their thievery the kind of small-time stuff for which a brutal government likes to exact vengeance and call it justice.

But if this is in fact the case, if they were in fact small-time thugs, it compels another observation as well; for when risks are great and rewards small, what would drive a man to a life of crime, if not desperation born of poverty? I don't know how these men's lives began, but I can guess that, given how they ended, they were not born to privilege; for when people of high estate deviate from the moral course, they tend to do so on a much grander scale, one befitting their station in life. They don't filch from widows but from pension funds. They don't pick pockets; they cook books. (As Jacques Brel observed, "Yes, robbing a bank is bad, but compared to owning one . . . ?"[3]) No, if I had to guess I'd say that these were two men who were born with little and died with less.

As thieves, they by necessity lived their lives in the shadows, no doubt knowing few people and trusting even fewer. They would not attach themselves to a community, for how could they see others as possible friends without first seeing them as potential prey? Like the jackals that roamed the Palestinian countryside by dark of night, they pledged allegiance only to themselves and taking the edge off their own hunger. Some days they'd get their hands on a little purloined coin or meat or cloth; other days luck would be against them and they would get nothing. But it is unlikely that these two-bit crooks ever hit the big score that would have let them live off the fat of their slaughter. It was a desperate, demeaning, lonely way of life that did little to nourish the body and much to starve the soul.

Ironically, then, the *one* day of their lives (the last) they were to garner attention, to be noticed by others, to be ignoble headliners on a rogue's stage, they are usurped by a man of pure innocence who neither deserves nor protests his fate. He is the one the crowd has come to see, not they; the thieves, again, are bit players in the human drama. Still in the shadows.

## The Choice Is Ours

We might think there was no common bond to be found between the thieves and their unlikely counterpart, but indeed there was this: whatever forces conspired to drive each one of them to do what they did with their lives, be it to relieve people of their money or their pain, human volition was the ultimate arbiter of those choices. This is an important acknowledgment, because it underscores the humanity of both the criminals and the Christ and thereby avoids the risk of caricaturing one and deifying the other. After all, choice is the sovereign faculty of the mind, to paraphrase

Thornton Wilder.[4] So, following Bonhoeffer's advice to his young couple, and to himself, let us not be too quick to hold God responsible for decisions Jesus freely made.

It was by choice that he cut against the grain of prevailing orthodoxy and preached a message of subversive love, so much so that he could find as much decency in the heart of a repentant prostitute as hypocrisy in the heart of a religious elitist. And it was by choice that he accepted the dangers that inhere in such a message. He knew that he could not bring freedom to the captives without experiencing the enmity of their captors, could not advocate for the peasants without inflaming the kings, could not raise the fortunes of the meek and lowly without lowering the fortunes of the high and haughty. As Dom Helder Camara, Brazilian archbishop of Olinda, once observed about the risks of such preaching, "When I feed the poor, they call me a saint, but when I inquire as to the reasons for their poverty, they call me a communist."[5]

Some say it was Jesus' destiny, and perhaps it was. But what is destiny, if not a conspiracy between those forces over which we have no control and those forces over which we do? We are not all

---

A friend of mine is an influential and generous alumnus of his university, so when his daughter, Rebecca, was accepted into the following year's freshman class, he could not have been more proud. But Rebecca's excitement was tempered by the nagging thought that she had, as she put it, "snuck in the back door," that she had been accepted not solely on her own merit but because of her father's prominence.

"I had an unfair advantage because of you," she told her dad, and he did not disagree.

"You're absolutely right," he answered, but then he added this indispensable wisdom: "You wake up every morning in the confines of a loving family, and that gives you an unfair advantage over some kids. You have a roof over your head, and you go to school on a full stomach, and that gives you an advantage over some other kids. Your mother and I can *afford* to send you to a good school, and that gives you an advantage over other kids. You have your health, and that gives you an advantage over some other kids.

"Rebecca, it's not about whether you've been given an advantage, because you have. The question is, what will you *do* with that advantage?"

given the same opportunities in life; some of us are born to poverty and others to privilege, some healthy and others infirm, some into loving families and others into fractious ones. And there is no philosophical sleight of hand that makes the unjust just. But I do not abide the notion that Jesus or anyone else is simply borne aloft on a breeze of human experience without providing some tilt to the direction they would have that breeze take them.

One thief recognized this and one didn't, and this made all the difference, because the one who did found an invitation to paradise. The good thief knew two things about himself—that the world had not been fair to him and that he had not been fair to it. Had circumstances been different, had he been born to a higher order or blessed with a rare and wonderful talent, then perhaps this day would have found him in the court of the king who issued his sentence, rather than on the cross with which it was carried out. But in the face of this arbitrary unfairness with which all lives are visited, he did not resort to pity or retreat to anger. When all else was lost, what he found was one man who chose to keep company with him. In the very depths of his aloneness, he was not alone.

While so many people had been drawn to Jesus because of the magnetism of his power—to heal, to preach, to rouse, to defy convention—this man was drawn instead by the grace of his powerlessness. As this unnamed man hung there, his ebbing life met by the indifference of the mob at his feet, receiving "the due reward of [his] deeds," he came to understand something. Like a beam of light before the gathering gloom, he saw in Jesus a man who, in choosing *not* to exert that power, not to protest his innocence, not to save but to willingly sacrifice himself for the sake of others, was offering by example the purest form of love—even to him. For perhaps the first time in his life, he was loved, so much that all he could do in response was confess his sins and plead for the forgiveness that was granted when Jesus assured him that on that day they would together enter paradise. Consoled by the knowledge that he would not die alone, he must have felt as though he already stood at its doorstep. For him, the last convert of Jesus' earthly ministry, death no longer held sway. Bound to his cross, he was a free man. Powerless to change his fate, he was fully and finally empowered to embrace it. Such a death, in the words of Hannah Arendt, bestows upon life "a silent completeness, snatched from the hazardous flux to which all things human are subject."[6]

## The Common Bond

Its extraordinary context in human history notwithstanding, this one moment in time between Jesus and the good thief is emblematic of the deepest, timeless yearnings of all our souls. For what do we want, if not to be loved despite our weaknesses and to love others despite theirs? Where is salvation to be found, if not there, where surrender meets assurance?

I remember finding myself in a small-town police station one night, years ago, waiting to visit a young man who had put himself in the wrong place at the wrong time with bad results. While I was biding my time, a fifteen-year-old boy named Charles, whose mother was on her way to pick him up, was brought out from the holding cell. Charles was being detained for hot-wiring a car and taking it for a joy ride. I learned from the desk sergeant that he was an otherwise good kid, had never been in trouble, had never given his parents reason to think he was destined for anything but a promising future. This was his first offense and, the sergeant suspected, would be his last.

When Charles's mother entered the precinct house, she did something that has stayed with me all these years. She went right over to him, took him by the arms, looked him in the eye, and with steady voice and steely gaze, said to him, "Son, listen to what I have to say. I love you. And I am so, so very angry at what you have done." She delivered both messages with equal conviction, and he was reduced to tears in her arms. *We alone bear the responsibility for what no one can take from us.*

Charles wept, not because he had broken the law, but because his mother's love was such that it rose above her anger at his transgression. She was furious with him and would punish him—no less compelling evidence of her devotion—but she was also quick to remind him that hers was not a love that could be bought or sold, that it was a permanent, immutable thing, that he was anchored in it, and that triumphs could not strengthen it or failures diminish it. I think of the many children I have met, some now grown into adulthood, who never felt such unconditional love, and I can't possibly enumerate the many ways they've suffered for being denied that love to which they were entitled. They are the ones who fought for the attention of a disinterested mother, who dreaded the repercussions of a middling report card, who struggled to make the team in a sport they didn't even want to play but did so because it would please dad. They are the ones who cried over spilled milk. Charles, I thought, was one of the lucky ones.

Such abiding, knee-weakening love as Charles enjoyed is not limited to the overriding of personal failures or moral lapses. One needn't have committed a crime to experience the humbling grace of unmerited love. In any situation or circumstance, however sad or hopeless, however helpless one person is to take away the pain of another, the burden of that pain can at the very least be shared and thereby lessened.

I think of a mesmerizing scene in Ingmar Bergman's *Cries and Whispers,* a story of the tangled relations between three sisters, in which one of the three, Agnes, suffering from cancer, flies into a rage of pain and panic. The other two try fruitlessly to gather her up and bring her under control, but she just spins deeper and deeper into her frenzy. Finally the maid, Anna, takes her quietly in her arms, like Giotto's Madonna in his *Lamentation over the Dead Christ,* and rests Agnes's head against her breast. By this one simple little gesture Agnes is soothed, and stroked, and quieted. It was as though Anna was telling her, "I cannot make you well again, but I can assure you that you are not alone in your suffering. On the deepest levels I can be with you, sit with you, flesh against flesh, with nothing separating us. And in this way I can love you, and you will know that wherever your fate takes you, my love will ride with you." Like Christ on the cross, the young maid is offering to this woman the promise that when all the externalities of life are stripped away, ultimately all we are left with is one another. But in our darkest moment, this will suffice. Death need not sting, nor need we fear it.

When we love others despite the circumstances of their lives or the specifics of their worst decisions, we are doing for them as Jesus did for the thief. We are permitting their frailties to remind us of our own and in so doing allowing compassion to transfigure empathy. We do this when we sit late at night at the side of the old man for whom fear is the prospect of death or the young child for whom it is the three-headed monster under her bed. We do it when we listen patiently to the tired screeds of the neighbor whom no one else will abide or the hangdog woes of a lonely-hearted pal. We also do it when we feed the poor *and* inquire as to the reasons for their poverty. That is to say, even when we can bring little more than our willingness to cleanse with our tears the wound that cannot be healed, we are at least approximating the love our thief found in full perfection on that sad afternoon so many years ago.

And conversely, when we sacrifice our *own* egos, confess our own fears and failings, and receive mercy from another, we are, like the good thief, allowing God to come into us in this way. As Henri Nouwen noted, "it is so much more blessed to give, but it is so much more difficult to receive."[7] This willingness to receive love is truly a moment of receiving God incarnate, in the form of a friend, a family member, or perhaps a complete stranger, who in that moment loves us not *because* of who we are but *regardless* of it.

Many years ago a Hungarian novelist by the name of Gyorgy Konrad wrote a book entitled *The Case Worker,* in which he drew upon his experiences as a children's social worker. In it, Konrad captured with eloquence the pain some children feel as dispensable commodities in a harsh society and the need to love them as they are. In addressing their hunger for love, he is addressing our own, for in his words, as in our hearts, we can find both the Christ and the thief:

> let all the children come, the babies abandoned in hospitals and nurseries, in doctors' offices and on strangers laps . . . let them all come, our unbidden, avenging enemies . . .
>
> let children from the institutions come, with their numbered underwear and vacant eyes; who wait behind bars for visitors who *never* come, whose tearful, pleading letters never bring an answer . . .
>
> let the eternal underdogs come, those whose ribs are crushed

year in and year out by the same steel spring . . . who through cellar windows see only the shoes of their fellow creatures . . . those around whom iron turns to rust, plaster crumbles and wood rots . . .

let the bungling mechanics come, those who can never put themselves together out of their component bits and pieces . . . the neglected who have never been given anything for nothing, the underprivileged whose wildest dream is to be next to the last . . . those who shuffle from one foot to the other and finally decide not to ring the bell after all, those with trembling lips who are never let in on the secret . . . whose hats get sat on . . . who are often asked how they are by people who are already walking away . . . who, wavering between disgust and indifference born of familiarity, can, in a privileged moment of tenderness, light the Christmas sparkler of mescaline-induced recognition and exalt the law of inalienable freedom above the experience of their own insignificance . . .

let all those come who want to; one of us will talk, the other will listen; at least we shall be together.[8]

We are to be found here, I believe, at both extremes. In the twilight hour of our uncertainty, when we are least wanted and of little use to anyone. When all we can do is supplicate, arms opened, cruciform, we are Konrad's unbidden child, his eternal underdog. We are the good thief, who wants only to know that as that twilight yields to darkness, we are not alone in this world. And in some other way, at some other place and time, when fortuity has us meet the supplicant whose dream it is to be *next* to last, who is asked how she is by people who are already walking away, we will not walk away. We will stay, and sit. We will love the rebellious child as only a brokenhearted parent can. We will hold her cancer-riddled body close to ours. We will give comfort and assurance to the good thief. One of us will talk, and the other will listen. At least we shall be together, this day, in paradise.

Thus is our choice, our sacred trust, *for we alone bear the responsibility for what no one can take from us.*

# Mary, the Mother of Jesus

*Mamma, mamma, many worlds I've come since I first left home.*

—Robert Hunter, for The Grateful Dead

*When Jesus saw his mother, and the disciple whom he loved standing near, he said to his mother, "Woman, behold your son!" Then he said to the disciple, "Behold your mother!" And from that hour the disciple took her to his own home.*

—John 19:26–27

$W$e pray to her, worship her, sanctify her, and venerate her. Christmas is not Christmas without our hearing her story, without hearing of the long ride out of Nazareth to Bethlehem, the fears of a first-time mother not yet wed, the dire warnings of Herod's retribution, the birth of her son in a stranger's barn, the lonely and unsettling sojourn in Egypt. And from these morsels we intuit much about this young woman who is called "the handmaid of the Lord," because in few places other than Jesus' birth stories is she even mentioned, let alone so prominently. The Mary of the Christmas story is a pillar of strength and stoic calm; she willingly endures the hardships of travel and faithfully accepts the news that in her womb she carries the one who will "reign over the house of Jacob for ever" and of whose "kingdom there will be no end." It is this woman, whose character is thus established in these early Gospel verses, that we see—or think we see—throughout the breadth of Jesus' ministry and at his feet at the moment of his death.

This being the case, it is easy to understand why we have memorialized her the way we have. When I think of how we depict Mary, what comes to my mind is the placid, almost serene resignation on her face in Michelangelo's *Pieta*. She is solid and silent there, like the marble from which she is carved. She is more the embodiment of a comforter than a grieving mother in need of comfort, hinting at no emotion save gentle love, even as her son lies dead in her arms. In her nobility she is so angelic as to border on the unapproachable.

I have no doubt that Mary was a woman of great dignity, or that she rose to the unique mantle that came with her motherhood, rather than shrank from it. I also believe she was as human as any of us, as capable of doubt as of faith, honored to have been so chosen, but also profoundly saddened by the destiny foretold for her son. Had she on any occasion cursed God for the burden she carried, I think God would have forgiven her. The Mary who bore the Savior in her womb and the crucified Lord in her arms is indeed a saint. But she is more. She is also a parent.

## Ordinary Enough

What commended Mary to God? By all indications she was not a woman of wealth or bearing, did not command legions of servants, was not educated or cultured. She was, in her own words, of "low estate." It is possible that she is a descendant of the house of David, but in the Palestine of her day this would be the equivalent of a tired old Austrian dowager today boasting a shared pedigree with the Hapsburgs. The connection is incidental and the significance of the lineage is long since past. So why such an ordinary mother for such an extraordinary child?

It is the ordinariness itself that made her such a logical choice to give birth to a king "of [whose] kingdom there will be no end," because this would be a kingdom like no other. It would be a kingdom of Marys and Josephs, of commoners and carpenters, and shepherds and innkeepers. It would be a kingdom described in parables of laborers and sowers, mustard seeds and fig trees, simple things that are wedded to the earth for their sustenance. It would not be a place where rule is imposed by might or where authority is derived from power. It would not be governed by politicians in the pockets of the rich, nor would it be a society whose policies are derived from, defined by, and beholden to persons of influence. As Jesus himself would later describe it, it would be a place where the widow's mite in the temple's coffer will be worth more than all the gold deposited by those of means whose showy offerings are little more than egotism masquerading as altruism. The kingdom whose seed first lay in Mary's womb would be a place where the despised are exalted and the reviled are esteemed; where the merciful would obtain mercy, the pure would see God, the hungry would be satisfied, and the meek would inherit the earth. It would, in short, be a world turned upside down.

With this in mind, who better to bring Jesus into that world than one who has lived on its harder edge? She would not pamper him because it would not be in her ethic or her budget. He would be forced to do chores and to live simply, and he would see the great disparities that separated people of means from people of need. When he walked with her to market, he would see how carefully she parceled out her dinarii, and how infrequently she would buy the stuff of fine meals. He would see extravagance reserved for holidays, and, deep into the night, when his parents thought him asleep, he would overhear them as they wondered aloud how they were going to meet this month's taxes.

Hers was the right world for him to be born into and raised in, because unlike other "kingdoms," this one came with no sense of entitlement, expectation, or bequest. This kingdom came instead with a notion of fairness and respect, of respectable living conditions, ample food, decent jobs, and freedom from want. It came with an image of economic and social equality that is as much a dream to people of modest means as it is a nightmare to people of great wealth (reminding me of Jefferson's admonition to the aristocracy of his day that they'd better be careful if they ask God for justice, because he just might give it to them). Jesus was well served to be raised in the austerity of Nazareth, because it would help him to appreciate the idea of justice from the standpoint of those who enjoyed little of it, rather than those who exercised little of it.

Perhaps the faded glory of the Davidic descent served Mary as well, for it was a cautionary tale to her young son, teaching him of the fickleness of political power. For kingdoms do fall, and from Egypt to Enron, it is not another empire or hard times that brings them down, but, more than anything else, it is hubris, a sense that power is the prerogative of those who hold it and will last forever. In this light, in the collapse of David's dynasty Jesus could appreciate what happens when the upstart with the slingshot eventually becomes no different from the Goliath he has slain. So perhaps it was not only his mother's humble surroundings but her glorious lineage and its tragic trajectory that informed Jesus' thought and work.

## Mother Mary

She was many things in her life and many more in her death, but above all else she was a parent. She was told before her son was born what destiny had in store for him, and surely throughout his life she thought often of this. Indeed, having learned of the great celestial events that surrounded his birth—the Lord appearing to Joseph in a dream, a star appearing to the wise men in the east, an angel appearing to the shepherds in the hillocks—Mary, we are told by Luke, "kept all these things, pondering them in her heart." But she was also a woman who nursed scraped knees and colic and paid attention to whether her son kept up his studies and who his friends were. She worried when he didn't come home before dark and chided him if he didn't look after himself. And just as all of us who are parents also want their children to do something worthwhile with their lives and stay safe from harm, and in the case of her son, the first would obviate the second.

She knew all this too, of course, because just days after the extraordinary events with which his life began, the righteous Simeon prophesied where it was headed, telling her, "This child is set for the fall and rising of many in Israel, and for a sign that is spoken against (and a sword will pierce through your own soul also)" (Luke 2:34–35). She knew that her son's life would be unlike any other's, that he was a gift not just to her but to the world, but it did not render her any less responsible to raise him right, and did not make her any less a mother in terms of the hopes and fears and dreams and love she harbored for her son. And by all indications, he being the product of her efforts, she was a remarkable parent.

One of the hallmarks of her parenting is also familiar to many of us: all the while that she was caring for and fretting about her young child, she knew he would not be hers forever. The one thing kids don't understand is that we parents continue to see them as our children long after they have stopped seeing us as their parents. It is our job to slowly loose the reins and let them find their way into the world, and it is their job to pull at those reins in search of their independence and their identity. When they find it they are free of us, but we are still bound to them; we can no longer direct their lives, but we are pledged lifelong to the unique vulnerability and concern we feel for their welfare and happiness.

> "A boy becomes an adult three years before his parents think he does, and about two years after he thinks he does."
> —Lewis B. Hershey

A young mother-to-be, Cathy, was in my office about six months' shy of her delivery date. Cathy was a thoughtful, contemplative woman with strong religious convictions and a deep respect for family. She also suffered from a mild anxiety disorder, something I thought might be more difficult for her to control now that she was about to feel the added anxiety of first-time parenthood.

That day we talked about her child's life, that his foremost responsibility, his calling, as it were, would be to grow up, to leave her and her husband, a little bit at a time. Whether it was with that first uncertain step, the first day of school, or the first apartment, the child would regularly be claiming for himself responsibilities his parents once held. Cathy took this in with great seriousness and

then asked anxiously, "When does it start?" "With your first con-
tractions," I told her. "Up until then, you will have been, among
other things, his lungs. The first thing he will insist is that he
breathe for himself." And from there on out, the reins only further
loosen. The love and concern of his parents would remain stead-
fast, but their power to control his life would inexorably diminish.

And so it was with Mary as it is with all of us. As her son grew
up and began to go off and find his way, she would wonder how
and when he would meet his great destiny, but at the same time she
would wonder too whether he had enough money to live on and
whether he steered clear of the sorts of roads where rogues and
thieves lay in wait. She was the Blessed Virgin Mother. But she
was also Mom.

And he doesn't seem to have made it easy on her, but instead
tugged harder on those reins than most children. When he was
twelve and in Jerusalem for the Passover, he wandered off without telling his parents where he was going, and after three days
that had to be as terrifying for Mary and Joseph as they would for
any of us whose child was missing in a strange city, they found
him holding forth in the temple. When, with anger mixed with
fear (mitigated by unimaginable relief), they asked him why he'd
done this to them, he answered not with an apology but with a
variation on a Hebrew psalm. "How is it that you sought me?" he
said to them. "Did you not know that I must be in my Father's
house?" In other words, if Jesus felt the least bit penitent for having put them through this ordeal of his unexplained disappear-
ance, he not only didn't show it; he let it be known that hereafter
his allegiance to his heavenly parent would supersede his allegiance to his earthly ones.

Later, at Cana, his mother now widowed, Jesus rebuked her
again, this time with the words, "O woman, what have you to do
with me? My hour has not yet come" (John 2:4). And later still,
when he was preaching to a large audience and his "mother and
brothers stood outside, asking to speak to him," he rebuffed them.
"Who is my mother, and who are my brothers?" he asked, rhetorically (Matt. 12:46–48). For to him his family was now synony-
mous with his following. I have no doubt that Mary, having "kept

all these things, pondering them in her heart" (Luke 2:19), understood, if sadly, that this was the price she paid for the gift she gave the world. But I also have no doubt it grieved her dearly. This child, whose journey into that world was wrought through her agony, an agony that was known to cost women their lives, this child who suckled at her breast and sat on her lap and learned at her feet, was no longer seeing her as his mother. She, on the other hand, to the day she died, would always see him as her son.

## Woman, Behold Your Son

It was at the foot of the cross that the grip of control that a parent holds over a child was loosed and the reins relinquished once and for all. It was the time of complete surrender, for Jesus to give up his life and for Mary to finally lose the foreboding that she had long lived with.

But they were not sharing an idle moment; it was time for Jesus to give Mary over to a disciple to be cared for and for Mary to become the mother of the church. That Mary was there is symbolic; she still thought of him as her child, long after he had stopped thinking of her as his parent. It was a mother's love, not a disciple's devotion, that called her there. On the other hand, it was *precisely* that devotion that brought "the disciple whom he loved"

Many years ago my sister gave birth to a child, a little girl she named Amy, whose life was destined to last only a matter of months. Because of severe genetic damage, Amy would never leave the hospital. Every day my sister would sit with her, and hold her in her arms, and, deep into the night, would talk to her with words the child would not grow to understand. The emotional toll was great, but when one of Amy's physicians suggested to my sister that she need not subject herself to this heartache day in and day out, and not allow herself to get so bound up with a child who had no future, she answered quite resolutely, "This is my daughter. And as long as she is alive, I am her mother. And this is what mothers do." Amy died having not experienced many things in life. No finger painting, no Sesame Street, no belly rubs or tosses in the air. But as we said our goodbyes to her, I could not help but think: she never experienced abandonment either.

there, to be at his feet and at her side. For what made this disciple beloved in Jesus' eyes was the fact that when all the others had suc- cumbed to their fears and taken flight, he was compelled by love to stay. He was, as the scholar Raymond Brown points out, the one who went with Jesus to the court of the high priest, which meant that at the very place where Peter, out of fear for his life, denied knowing Jesus, this man boldly stood with him. It was no accident, then, and no surprise, that at the moment of death "the disciple whom he loved" stood with Jesus still.

Nor was it an accident that Jesus' last act before his death was to join the two of them, saying to this unnamed disciple, "Behold your mother!" In this one gesture he united his mortal life with his anointed one. The mother Jesus had at times kept at arm's length, the woman he had rebuked for the concern she showed him, he now showed concern for, and attended to that concern by uniting her with this man. Jesus' mother, the one person who fully embraced his humanity and treated him as any parent would her child, is joined together with the one person who fully embraced— for all of the dangers it promised—his divinity. In the disciple Jesus had found the man who would show Mary the same abiding devotion he had shown his Lord. And in Jesus' instruction to this disciple, the son became the father: Jesus' love for Mary was now fatherly, a direct reflection of the love she always held for him, even when Jesus turned away from it. This protective, parental love sought only to know that she would be all right, that she would be safe. She would need the unnamed disciple, Jesus knew, just as he would need her as he went forth to do God's work. Because, as Jesus realized, he too could not have done his work without her. And with that, Jesus' work was done. His ministry had run its course and been brought to its conclusion. And he could now slip off to death, in the words of the evangelist, "knowing that all was now finished."

The truth is, Jesus and Mary were more alike than either may have ever imagined: they were both anointed to a divine calling, both bore secrets that were the product of that calling, both knew of the inevitable suffering that awaited, and both possessed the strength to face it with courage and calm. And perhaps this kinship is what nudged him away and what brought him back, for children must find their own identities, rather than simply mirror those of their parents. But, once having done so, they can then permit themselves to find a place in their hearts for that parent without fearing that they themselves will be consumed by the intimacy. Only in establishing their hard-fought independence from home can they return to it knowing that their affection for the place and the people in it does not jeopardize their sense of freedom from it.

And so it was quite fitting that in his last moments on earth Jesus saw to it that his mother had a home to go to, just as he now went to his.

In the final analysis what makes Mary so very special is not that she bore this child but that she raised him. She allowed herself to love him as only a parent can love a child: fiercely, unconditionally, with every breath of her life and every fiber of her being. She held him close when closeness was what he needed, and when it was time to let him go, she did this too. She is every parent who relishes the joy and endures the heartache that comes with this territory, and in her story the admiration I feel toward the Mary who was an instrument of God is equaled only by the admiration I feel toward the Mary who was a mother.

# The Centurion

*A state of conscience is better than a state of innocence.*
—Thomas Mann

*When the centurion, who stood facing him, saw that he thus breathed his last, he said, "Truly this man was the Son of God."*
—Mark 15:39

Where do our principles and values come from? Our beliefs and ethics? Our raison d'être?

The young boy soaks up all manner of information and stimulus, and he takes it in with little discrimination concerning what is important and what is not. Over time he begins to sort it out and sift it through a filter that is largely the product of his accumulating life experiences, with a pinch of DNA thrown in. Slowly, gradually, his priorities emerge, and they eventually provide a basis for his values. His trust in others is sometimes validated and sometimes violated, and these experiences in time become a foundation for a belief system. He engages in a wide variety of deeds and actions; some prove to be less than satisfying, while others give him an enormous sense of fulfillment. The sum total of his experiences then serves as the bedrock for his vocation, his sense of calling, the marriage of labor to love.

In his formative years, he goes through many changes in thought and heart, but eventually arrives at a set of core beliefs by which he conducts his affairs. He has friends who live only on the

surface of their lives, but he begins to take his beliefs more seriously, more self-consciously and more deeply.

This is a journey many of us take.

But what happens when something intrudes on our assumptions, penetrates our core, shakes it, and threatens to be its undo-
ing? What is it like to experience something so overpowering that
we are forced to question what a lifetime of seeking has brought
us to believe in? What was it like for the centurion?

## Caesar's Apologist

He was the commanding officer of a "century," one hundred foot
soldiers in Caesar's army. In all likelihood he was himself a career
soldier, well paid and well regarded. His was a noble order who
were expected to impose a certain stability on their ranks and to
pledge their undying fealty to the emperor. The historian Polybius
wrote of centurions, "They are required . . . to be good leaders, of
steady and prudent mind . . . able, when overwhelmed and hard-
pressed, to stand fast and die at their post."[1] With the prospect of
death as a constant companion, this was not a career one chose
lightly or pursued without great sacrifice.

The centurion at the cross was a Gentile, which meant he was
far from home. He was among people who had their homeland
taken from them by an occupying force, and he was a part of that
force, so that he lived with the constant danger of political revolt.
He did not speak the language of the Jews or know their customs,
which only underscored his outsider status and stirred his long-
ings for his native land. To endure the dangers and hardships
attendant to a career such as his, he had to believe in who he was
as a warrior and what he did as a protector of the empire. So what
happened?

## Dark Disturbing Doubts

He and his men had likely been in Jerusalem at least long enough
to understand the controversy surrounding Jesus' ministry, for sol-

diers new to the environs would not have been given as highly charged an assignment as this particular crucifixion. He likely knew at least the fundaments of Jesus' teaching and certainly had a feel for the intensity of sentiments generated by both his supporters and his detractors.

As the days before the crucifixion dwindled down and passions heated up, his work would become more consuming; at the same time he would come to have a better, more informed appreciation for the character and sincerity of the man his empire had put on trial. He would see that the case against Jesus was flimsy and the trial a mockery of justice. He'd see too that the governor even gave the man an opportunity to escape with his life and that the man believed so strongly in the rightness of his cause that he refused the offer. If the events of those days triggered sporadic riots in the streets—as well they may have—he would have been struck by the man's call for calm and his appeal to his followers to remember that those who live by the sword die by it. And as Jesus proceeded to his death, as he accepted his cross, his crown, his fate with such unimaginable dignity, whatever battle had been waged for the soul of this soldier, who for years *had* lived by the sword, was finally won in that moment when his greatest adversary surrendered his last breath. And so much of what he believed in, so much of what he stood for as a Roman and as a warrior, surrendered itself as well.

There were those who for years observed Jesus' ministry, only to conclude that it was either too fantastic or too dangerous to believe in. Others had their doubts but slowly shed them and, over time, came first to consider his message, then to accept it, and then truly to live by it. They were the hard-won converts for whom faith slowly wended its way from their heads to their hearts (or perhaps vice versa) and took root. And then there was the centurion, and perhaps others like him, whose beliefs could not have been more antithetical to those of the Jews, who knew less of Jesus than anyone else, and who stood to lose more than everyone. His is the conversion of pure and unbridled enthusiasm—*en theos*, to be with God. It was not a decision he came to logically; it was one of overwhelming emotion.

The centurion was compelled to his conversion, not *because* of all he had come to believe in in his years of service to the Roman Empire, but *despite* it. After all, central to that empire's assumption of its own legitimacy as an imperialist force was the idea that the emperor himself was God's emissary on earth. What greater affront to the emperor himself could the centurion have made than to refute such a conceit? He voiced his rejection of the supremacy of the empire at great peril, and if after this one outburst he continued to profess Jesus as the child of God, he would do so with the loss of his livelihood a certainty and the loss of his life a distinct possibility.

## From Here, Where?

But we know nothing about the subsequent chapters in the centurion's life. We'd like to believe that, like Paul on the road to Damascus, his witness to the crucifixion was enduring; that it truly and irrevocably changed his life. We'd like to think that he was a new being, that the power of God revealed to him in the figure of Christ on the cross cleanly pierced his soul and made it impossible for him to revert to his old gods. What wonderful symbolism it would make: a man of war is won over by the Prince of Peace. A pagan accepts the God of Abraham. A career soldier risks his life by rejecting the empire to which he once pledged his undying allegiance. It would be a tale for the ages, an affirmation of the primacy of God and a testimony of the redemptive power of the crucifixion. But we just don't know.

It may be well and good to be left in the dark on this, because the uncertainty forces us to ponder the fragile nature of conversion, how even the most heartfelt can be more sincere than durable. Perhaps the drama of the moment touched some deeply hidden vein of unhappiness that this centurion had long suppressed. It's not beyond the pale to imagine that here may have been a man who, over years of service, had grown disillusioned with his allegiance to the cause of the empire. Perhaps he had seen one too many friends die by the enemy's sword, had been passed over once too often for a promotion, had grown tired of the resentments con-

quered people heap on occupying armies, or had come to question
the morality of empire building itself. Perhaps killing no longer
agreed with him.

But perhaps too with the passage of time, he would come to
weigh his unhappiness against the knowledge that life is often a
series of compromises. He was a soldier and a servant of the realm.
It was what he did, what he knew, what rewarded him and his family. It kept a roof over their heads and food in their bellies. In the final
analysis, what difference does one god make over another, he may
have thought, when all you're trying to do is live your life and take
care of your own? And so perhaps his moment of clarity and certainty washed over him like a great wave, but then receded, as waves
do, taking a bit of sand with it, leaving the ground beneath his feet a
little unsure, if only for a while. And in short order he would revert
again to his life of accomplishment and accommodation.

If he did retreat in this way, he wasn't the first, nor would he be
the last, to make such a brave proclamation, only to back away
from it when the heat of the moment cooled to a memory. I think
of recovering drug addicts and alcoholics I have worked with who,
soon out of detox, declare themselves fully reborn. They've found
Jesus, they may tell me, and they're going to spend the rest of their
days serving their Lord. They'll never lose another job, never miss
another child support payment, never pick another fight over a bag
of weed or a fifth of whiskey. Only in time do they learn how steep
the climb really is, this ascent they must make every day of their
lives toward a summit—certain sobriety for the rest of their
lives—they will never reach. They see how littered the path is with
the wreckage of good intentions and how easy it is to slip and fall.
Most of them don't stay in recovery, which isn't to say they didn't
mean it when they declared themselves clean and dry, only that
they could not appreciate how difficult it is to renounce one set of
habits and values for another.

But I also think of quieter, less sensational ways that conversions—little conversions, the ones that lack the centurion's
drama—grow old and stale. I look around the church sanctuary on
Easter Sunday or Christmas Eve, the place bulging with righteous
strangers, and wonder whether, when they sing "O come, all ye

faithful," they will indeed come next week, or when they proclaim, "Christ is risen indeed!" they will do so not only as a celebration of life but as a pledge to pick up the work left undone on that first Easter morning. As Henry Nouwen once said, "From the empty tomb we hear the call, 'Go to Galilee!' "[2]

I think of the many professionally successful patients I have had whose laments were that they were too busy making a living to have a life. They wanted to give their children the time they deserved, but after a couple weekends of ballgames and trips to the merry-go-round, they often reverted to old form and in so doing only intensified their kids' sense of cynicism.

Or I think of how we behave outside of our families, in our communities. News comes down of a spike in poverty in our town or a family displaced by fire. We hear or read about the poverty and are compelled to rethink the way we spend our money, but only until it dawns on us that for a little extra cash we can get the leather seats for the new car or that big-screen TV for the playroom, and other people's problems really can't be our own. We want to change, we really do, but the desire to live a committed life is not always as strong as the temptation to lead a comfortable one. Or, to look at the story another way, we know the prodigal son came home. But did he stay? We do not know, of course, any more than we know if the centurion stayed.

But maybe he did. Many do. Take, for instance, the British renegade John Newton, whose conversion story has taken on almost folkloric proportions. Newton was an eighteenth-century slave trader who in 1748, while crossing the Atlantic on a slave ship called *The Greyhound*, ran into a fierce storm. After over a week battling the torrents of wind and rain, many among the exhausted and dispirited crew were certain all was lost. But they were wrong, and by what Newton believed to be the grace of God they eventually found land and safe harbor.

The experience left him transformed, and while he stayed in the business a short while longer, he eventually left slave trading, became a vocal abolitionist, received his ordination, ministered to London's poor, and memorialized his journey from a peddler of human beings to a servant of God in a hymn he titled "Amazing

Grace." Many years after his conversion, near death, Newton summed up his life this way: "My memory is nearly gone, but I remember two things: That I am a great sinner, and that Christ is a great savior."[3] The prodigal Newton came to God. And he stayed.

As has Mansour al-Nogaidan. Mansour, a small, cherubic-looking man with soft eyes and a gentle smile, was born and raised in the Saudi Arabian town of Buraida, in the heartland of extreme Islamic fundamentalism. After a rather unremarkable childhood, Mansour was drawn into the teachings of Osama bin Laden and the belief that Islam had to be purged of the corrupting influences of the West and that violence was the ultimate means for doing that. He became a hard-core extremist imam, preached hatred, and participated in firebombings. But at some point the seed of self-reflection found its way into his heart, and Mansour began to ponder both the wisdom and the morality of what he was espousing. In a land resistant to change, he changed and now sees himself as a reformist. "Saudi Arabia is bogged down by deep-rooted Islamic extremism," he wrote, encouraging his fellow citizens to "see ourselves the way the rest of the world sees us—a nation that spawns terrorists."[4] He wants to see his nation freed of corruption, cleansed of violence, and open to the idea that different cultures can live in harmony with one another.

For this Mansour has been censored, jailed, and beaten. And precisely because of this kind of rebuke, he has no choice but to carry on. Mansour is home, and he is staying.

## Forever Unfinished Business

The invitation to make new lives for ourselves can come to us in ways both sudden and sublime, in shouts and in whispers. More important than how that invitation is delivered is how we open ourselves to its possibility. We must have faith that God can speak to us through any medium, that we are works in progress, and that our lives are always worthy of examination. We also must understand that conversion is not a destination, an end point, but a journey *that has no destination*. We have not finished the task when we have received a new life, any more than the tilled soil produces the plant immediately upon receiving the seed. The real measure of the authenticity of our new life is what we do with it over time. What will it mean to us when that new life becomes old, when the thrill of concep-tion gives way to the hard work of gestation and of bringing it into fruition? How

> "Conversion for me wasn't a Dam-ascus Road experience. I slowly moved into an intellectual accep-tance of what my intuition had always known."
> —Madeleine L'Engle[5]

will we care for it against all countervailing pressures and seduc-tions? These are of course questions without a single answer, because in truth we are called upon to answer them not once, but every day of our lives.

Not a day goes by when we have respite from the need to decide whether our life will allow for the prospect that God will be made known to us. And when that happens, it is also ours to decide what to do with that knowledge. We can always let it in to make its claim upon us. We can always choose to hear the revealed word, however faint, to be a better people, to be more trusting that God's will might also be our own. The word becomes flesh when we choose to feed a hungry infant in a faraway land or tutor an inner-city child not blocks from where we live. It happens when we shed our long-standing indifference and raise a protest against the gloom of war, the despo-liation of the environment, or the abrogation of human rights by our government or other governments. It is also God's word that tells us it is better to miss the board meeting than the school play, that hon-esty trumps guile, and that apologies are the best alibis when we have wronged the ones we love. If only we listen, we will hear what the theologian Dietrich Bonhoeffer called "the cost of discipleship," the chance to choose conversion, to assess—in every waking moment—whether our values are in accord with God's and what, if anything, we are going to do with that assessment. Do we ally our-selves with our Caesar or with our Christ?

## Wherever Two or More Are Gathered

Finally, conversion is a matter not just of personal value but of public virtue. We do not live in isolation but in partnerships, and we need to remember that decisions made by a few can affect the many. When I worked in a small town in Connecticut, a group of activists tried to establish a safe house there for abused women. Though their efforts were initially met with pockets of pitched resistance in the politically conservative town, over time the village elders came around and—if begrudgingly on the part of some—allowed the house's doors to open. Now, some years out, the center not only meets a critical regional need; it also serves as one component of the collective moral identity of the town. For me the people who launched the campaign have always represented the irrupting, disrupting quality of conversion, the need to release old prejudices and welcome new principles. By extension, the town's reluctant willingness to open their doors is emblematic of the internal struggle that comes when the prospect of change is fully upon us. And the subsequent harmony that has ensued symbolizes for me the creative prospects of the conversion experience, the new being, the sweet sound of amazing grace.

This amazing grace may come when a community of believers, through the rigors of prayer and the discipline of self-reflection, opens itself daily to the ways in which it can be a more faithful emissary of the divine intention. And even entire nations, wrestling with the mighty issues of our time—the stewardship of their resources, the integrity of their leadership, their responsibility to other lands, their compassion toward the poor—are afforded the opportunity to nurture an ethos in which the greatness of the nation is derived from the goodness of its people.

So we don't know what happened to the centurion after he made his confession, any more than we can say with certainty whether—as individuals or collectively—our own efforts to think of ourselves in new ways will endure what John Newton called the "many dangers, toils, and snares" with which the world will present us. But we do know that the invitation, once extended, is never revoked. Our conversion to a life of true faith is less an episode than an ongoing process, a challenge we may gladly engage every day of our lives.

# 12

# The Women of the Cross

*Women who try to follow Christ do not challenge the church and the world for status, but seek ways to minister to both.*

—Jean Oddy[1]

*There were also women looking on from afar, among whom were Mary Magdalene, and Mary the mother of James the younger and of Joses, and Salome, who, when he was in Galilee, followed him and ministered to him; and also many other women who came up with him to Jerusalem.*

—Mark 15:40–41

*T*here were also women looking on from afar." What might the crucifixion have looked like from a distance? We can speculate with some confidence that in the thick of the drama and at the height of the hour, hundreds, if not more, clamored, cheek by jowl, to witness the great event. Believers wept while critics cheered. Rebels raised their fists in impotent rage but did little more, while the hesitant stood in awe, stunned at the drama but not yet sure about what it might mean to them or to their country. Temperatures, decibels, and passions all spiraled upward to create what must have been an intoxicating scene, the air redolent with wonder and pungent with dread. But what did it look like from afar?

I think of these three women, the two Marys and Salome, protecting themselves from all the madness, removing themselves to a place where the events unfolding atop Calvary would be no less real but much more muted. Where they could observe, take it in, without being overwhelmed by it. Where they could be with one another, give moral support to one another if need be, speak and be heard, or just sit in reverent silence, communicating through gesture or nod, "by quiet natures understood."[2] Women do this so much better than men. There was something very sad but very sane from that distant vantage. No histrionics, no hysteria. Just watching, keeping their lookout, with complete intensity, utter devotion, silent pain, and resignation. The distance was not an uncommon place for them, I suspect, because the Gospels themselves suggest that most of the women in Jesus' time were assigned to live on the periphery while the men fought to share center stage.

## Women in a World Run by Men

Indeed, women served Jesus with great but quiet loyalty. Luke's Gospel tells us of the one the evangelist simply identifies as "a sinner" who comes to where Jesus is having supper, wordlessly kneels before him, and in a moment of profound tenderness anoints his feet with her tears (Luke 7:36–50). Luke also observes that three other women—Mary, Joanna, and Susanna—contributed to Jesus' ministry, "provided for them out of their means" (Luke 8:1–3), even though they were not counted among his disciples. And in John we find the story of Lazarus's sisters, who create for Jesus a great meal in thanks for his healing their brother.

What emerges from these Gospel stories is a picture of women who sought first to offer their gratitude to Jesus, and yet in each of these stories I am left with the impression that they did so in a way that was not obsequious (as gratitude can sometimes appear from people who are giving extravagant thanks for something for which they feel so very undeserving) but bespoke their dignity and grace. I also believe Jesus recognized their dignity and made it easier for them to exhibit it. First-century Palestine was a hard place for a woman to feel fully enfranchised as a human being, to feel as though her intelligence, wisdom, and strength were appreciated. It was a patriarchal society in the sense that it was largely run by men. Men held positions of power in government and commerce. Men were widely regarded as the heads of their households. Levitical laws favored men in matters legal and marital. Women were responsible for bearing and raising children and for keeping their homes, but they had little power to make decisions that affected those homes, let alone their village or country. Women served at the pleasure of men in almost every respect. But precisely because it was a culture dominated by men, Jesus' was a presence that could be trusted; because he did not demand from them the servility that other men may have demanded. Then when they did show kindness and generosity to Jesus, they could do so freely.

Perhaps their relationship with Jesus was such a comfortable one for them because Jesus loved them in a way that no other men did. He healed them and their children of their illnesses. He forgave them their sins and bade them—for their own sake and self-respect—to sin no more. When he met the woman at the well—a Samaritan, who had slept with many men—he reproached her (had he met the men, he would have reproached them too), but he also taught her in a manner that respected her intelligence and afforded her hope. Jesus saw in women a beauty that went beyond their physical appearance to something deeper and more durable. He saw the strength to give birth to six children so that three might live, and the patience to stifle anger when men would deny them

Lot's wife gets a bad rap. She was told not to look back at the destruction of Sodom, and she did. And God punished her by making of her a pillar of salt. But what did she have to look *forward* to? She broke the rules, but when had the rules ever benefited her? If she were regarded as a full human being, with rights and privileges equal to men, why wasn't she given a name? Why was she defined only in relation to a man to whom she was married, as if a possession, like a piece of furniture or a beast of burden? Maybe it wasn't the weakness of curiosity that made her turn around that day, but the strength of independence that comes in those instances when we can say, "What do I have to lose?" If I could write the story, I think I would give her a name. I think it would be Gabriella. It is derived from the Hebrew word for strength.

their right to give voice to an original idea. He also saw them willing to sacrifice their own needs to those of their families, and he saw in his own mother a willingness to make the greatest sacrifice that faith has ever demanded of anyone. And if he was perceptive enough, he may well have observed the regard women held for one another for having been born women in a world run by men who didn't always do a particularly good job of it.

## Life from the Center On Out

Most societies are organized in concentric circles of power and influence, and the inner one is where many of the major decisions that will affect that society are made. That inmost circle is often populated by people of money and high status. It might include high-ranking government officials, holders of the public purse, bankers, industrialists, military leaders, social commentators, and opinion makers. Other circles are then occupied by people of progressively less power: radiating out from the core we would find, at various distances and in no particular order, government functionaries, midlevel executives, common laborers, unemployed workers, retirees, people of physical or psychological handicap, students, children, poor people, ex-convicts, and so forth, until we hit the outermost edge, those in the society who would be deemed, for all intents and purposes, the utterly powerless.

By cultural dictum the women in Jesus' life lived "at a distance" from the seats of power and influence, in the outer circles of Palestinian society. They were not divorced from the world, but perhaps because of the second-class status that was imposed on them, their motivation for doing what they did for him was also not compromised by a thirst for primacy and supremacy that overcame so many men. Their disposition was to live lives of service for service's sake. They were not driven by a need to elevate their status by appearing good in the eyes of others. Their lives were the lives of the humble—literally, those "of the earth"—of people who held no pretensions of eminence, influence, or wealth. And Jesus understood the purity and clarity in all of this.

For our era the truth is that most of us are—at least a good bit of the time—peripheral players, participating from a distance, and it's from there, from that place where we are *not* people of great importance, that we can emulate the women of the cross by doing good things for the mere sake of doing them. Like them, we can look to serve those around us who are in need of what we might have to offer. We can help to lighten another person's load, bring joy to someone whose existence may be joyless, or bind the wounds of an individual for whom no one is left to bind them. And we can do this, not as a means to elevated status, but as an end in itself, because, to paraphrase Matthew's gospel, By doing it for the least of our brothers or sisters, we are doing it for Jesus.

So perhaps the women looked on from a distance because it was a familiar place for them. It was familiar because they had been there before, countless times, because it was where they lived and where they served, but also because this is where *Jesus* was most at home, where his ministry was felt in its fullest measure. It is the refuge of the ordinary, of people for whom statues will *not* one day be erected in their honor and who may dream of wealth but then wake up to the reality that the rent is due. It is where somebody's neighbor was a face in the crowd in a photograph in the local newspaper, and now extra copies must be purchased for the folks who live out of town. It is the world where leisure might be a two-week vacation from the plant and extravagance a bungalow at the lake. It is ordinary lives whose greater significance is not automatically appreciated by the greater culture of which they are a part.

## Edmund and His Poverty of Purpose

When I think of where we find purpose in the living of those ordinary lives—in the doing of good for one another and the reciprocal pleasure that can bring—I think not only of how important it is that we do that; I think as well of one man in particular who taught me how devastating it can be if that sense of purpose is not realized.

His name was Edmund, and he lived, in his words, "on the edge of the edge," a place the women of the cross might have considered the farthest distance from that cultural core. Edmund was weather-worn and looked a decade older than his fifty-two years, with a face of many crevices and few teeth, matted hair, and perpetual stubble on his cheeks and neck. The product of many years living on the streets of New York City, he was a panhandler who never pretended to be anything else and would tell you as much. He worked a small stretch of blocks on upper Broadway and, when business was slow, would come by my office at the church to see if I could finesse a few bucks out of one budget or another. One rainy afternoon, want-ing either to hold forth or stay dry, Edmund was particularly expan-sive and described one facet of life on the edge of the edge.

"I don't mind being poor," he began, "because I don't want much. But you know the toughest part for me?" No, I didn't, but I guessed to myself it was the privation and hardship. I guessed wrong.

"It's standing on a corner in the morning, hat in hand, looking for enough money for a cup of coffee or a smoke. People are walk-ing by, this way and that." He paused a moment, looked up at the ceiling, and continued. "It's them. It's their walking that really gets to me. And do you know why?" Before I could even shrug my shoulders, Edmund answered his own question. "Because every-one's going *somewhere*, Rev! Everyone has somewhere they have to be. An appointment, a class, an office, a breakfast . . . *a purpose*. I could stand there all f***ing day and it wouldn't matter! That's the toughest part for me, Rev; there's no place I have to be. No one's waiting for me to show up. I got no purpose, man, no purpose."

Hanging out, hanging on, on the edge of the edge. I have to believe that if Jesus were alive today, he would sit with Edmund for a while, on any street corner, in any city. He would sit even if there *was* someplace he had to be, some higher purpose he had to serve. I believe he would talk with Edmund—not preach to him, but talk with him. And he'd listen to Edmund as well. He might tell him that even though he lives on the periphery while the ringmas-ters are busy occupying center stage, there is purpose to his life as well, that he is a good man and he might do well to figure out what that purpose is. Then maybe they would break bread together, and then be on their way.

Jesus' conversation with Edmund seems so natural in my

mind's eye because Edmund is the kind of company Jesus kept. It was the life he was born into and never really strayed from. He kept company with those of modest means and quiet lives whom others might not notice, and those of broken body and addled mind whom others worked very hard not to notice. There were the indigents with no shoes and the urchins with no parents, the elderly whose dwindling days are too swiftly gone, and the lonely, in their empty beds, whose nights are too long in passing. And there were the women. Looking on from a distance, there were the women.

As Jesus hung on his cross and looked out upon the crowd, his eyes slowly closing and his ears growing deaf to the mob's cries, I take solace in thinking that with one last surge of strength he lifted his head, looked to the horizon, and saw them. He would know that for them his crucifixion was not a spectacle, but a vigil. Not only would they not abandon him in his last moments of life; they would minister to him in death. He knew that when all others left the mountaintop, racked with guilt but oblivious to their responsibility, the women would take care of his body. They would see that it was removed from the cross, and they would take it to a tomb, anoint it, wrap it in linens, and lay it to rest in a proper way. And he would be overcome with a sense of peace, knowing that they loved him this thoroughly and this certainly. This is the love he died for; it is his bequest. And in the women's work, that love remains alive and becomes their inheritance.

This is why, when they returned to the tomb on the third day, in order that they might minister to him again by anointing his body with sweet spices, they were the first to know that the tomb was empty. When our faith becomes our work, when we give ourselves to it as selflessly as did those women, the resurrection breaks in upon us. Love does remain alive, despite all efforts to kill it.

## Life amid Death

I think of a day that changed my city and my life forever. What was it but the power of love that found life amid death, that turned ordinary men and women into heroes on that September morning in 2001? Everyone knew the casualties would be great, but we also knew that all morning long people were putting themselves in harm's way, often for complete strangers. Only later did we learn of some of their stories.

In the upper floors of the north tower, for instance, there were the two anonymous office workers, rushing down many flights of stairs, who spotted a woman in a wheelchair, and, without saying a word to one another, went to her, picked her up by her chair, and carried her down with them. At the same time, in an old building immediately adjacent to the site and itself threatening to collapse, there was Ada Dolch, a woman of modest stature but indomitable spirit who treated her job as a sacred calling. Ada was the princi-pal of a public school housed in the old structure and had to see to it that her kids were kept safe. Starting at the top floor and work-ing her way down, Ada engineered the safe escape of every single child and adult, all the while knowing that her sister had gone to work that morning on the eighty-eighth floor of the near tower and had likely not survived. Ada, though, could not let her grief for her sister impinge on her mission for her children. And then there was Mychael Judge, a colleague of mine, a Roman Catholic priest who served as chaplain to the New York City Fire Department. Mychael died because he was on site giving last rites to the fallen firefighters to whom he had ministered for so many years. Mychael was the first member of the department to lose his life that day, and, I sus-pect, would not have wanted to leave this earth any other way.

That night as we learned more about people's heroism, a friend said, "When the buildings went down and the smoke went up, the air above us was thick with angels." As the days wore on and I began to read the biographies of some of those angels, I was struck by how otherwise unextraordinary many of their lives seemed. They were lives of unassuming pleasures, noble dreams, backyard barbecues, and little fanfare. I read of many people who in all their days never saw the spotlight shine on them, who spent so much of their time far away from center stage, but who, at least through the eyes of this biased New Yorker, on this particular day became the most impor-tant people on the face of the earth. What more likely kind of per-sons to rise to the occasion than ones who otherwise spent a good portion of their lives not in halls of government or seats of power, not in jobs of great recompense or influence, but looking on from afar? There were many heroes that day, from every walk of life. But what I find particularly instructive and inspiring was the heroism of the secretaries, busboys, firefighters, cops, receptionists, and custodians who lost their lives or saved the lives of others because they did what *any of us* could do, for each one of us has the power to love other people in this way. However ordinary, however unexceptional our achievements in this world, God has given us that power. The question is only whether at any moment we have the will. And that is not God's decision, but our own.

Sometimes, when I think about it hard enough, I can in my mind's eye even imagine Edmund dropping his cup, letting the coins spill and not giving them a second thought, asking no favors, and dashing headlong toward the flames, toward his purpose. On this day, he would have lost that sense of insignificance that dogged him, and he too would have been counted among the most important people on earth. He would have been an angel.

But angels would not be angels if they did not work in more obscure ways as well, and many of those heroes had heroism writ small in their lives in ways most of us would otherwise never have known. For among them were Little League coaches and volunteers at their local food pantry, den mothers and deacons, foster fathers and candy stripers. They were people who sought simply to be of some purpose and who, when faced with their moment, did not retreat from it. The valor they exhibited when called upon to do so may have been there in their lives all that time, in these small and seemingly inconsequential ways.

When the cleanup was done, the great bustling expanse that was the World Trade Center became little more than a deep hole defined by sadness and stone, an empty tomb. But like the one the women returned to on that first Easter morning, if you listen carefully enough, you hear the echoes. They tell us that those we seek are not there—and that love conquers death.

# 13

# Joseph of Arimathea

*Life ought to be a struggle of desire toward adventures
whose nobility will fertilize the soul.*

—Rebecca West[1]

*Now there was a man named Joseph from the Jewish town
of Arimathea. He was a member of the council, a good and
righteous man, who had not consented to their purpose
and deed, and he was looking for the kingdom of God.
This man went to Pilate and asked for the body of Jesus.
Then he took it down and wrapped it in a linen shroud, and
laid him in a rock-hewn tomb, where no one had ever yet
been laid.*

—Luke 23:50–53

We know certain things about Joseph and can infer others; taken
together, they give us a picture of a man of high standing whose
influence could marry generosity to noble end. For example, having sought his fortune in the big city, he had become a man of
enough means not only to purchase a private tomb (a sure sign of
wealth in first-century Palestine) but to give it away. He was also
a wise man who was held in sufficient esteem to be appointed to
the Sanhedrin, a deliberative body whose job it was to govern the
Jews of Palestine and adjudicate civil and religious matters. He
was also an independent thinker, who did not always vote in accor-
dance with the rest of the Sanhedrin. He was a pious man as well,
evidenced by his wish to see Jesus' body buried in part to fulfill a
Jewish law that required executed criminals to be entombed within

twenty-four hours of death. And, having convinced Pilate to turn over the body of this political prisoner whom the Romans had just put to death, Joseph was in all likelihood a man of formidable influence, good with words and respected by a governor who was notoriously averse to controversy.

But there was one thing Joseph was not. He was not content. He was not satisfied. Despite being a man of riches and high regard, a man of personal piety and persuasive skill, what he sought above all else, as the evangelist puts it, was the *kingdom*. And by seeking he was not so much trying to discover its location as to define its content. As the essayist Roger Rosenblatt put it, "When you're wending your way down the river in search of truth, you hear faint whispers of it, and you know where it is. It is around the next bend. But that's precisely the problem. It's *always* around the next bend."[2] For Joseph to find the kingdom meant for him to know not where it is but what it is, what is around that next bend.

## The Unsettled Arimathean

Was the kingdom the Edenic valleys that the oracle Balaam described in the book of Numbers that "stretch afar, like gardens beside a river" (24:6)? Or was it a new and powerful empire, the kind the God of the exodus promised when he told the landless Hebrews, "If you will obey my voice . . . you shall be to me a kingdom of priests and a holy nation" (Exod. 19:5–6)? Perhaps it was neither; perhaps it was the metaphoric refuge Jesus described, where, like a mighty tree, "the birds of the air come and make nests in its branches" (Matt. 13:32). Or perhaps the kingdom was, in reparation for their poverty, the domain of the poor, the ones Jesus referred to in Luke when he proclaimed, "Blessed are you poor, for yours is the kingdom of God" (Luke 6:20).

So, as these uncertainties danced in his head and tugged at his heart, Joseph lived the life of a seeker. His search for the kingdom was not an isolated curiosity but was emblematic of a man who was forever unsettled. A more sedentary man, for instance, might never have left his sleepy town for the vagaries and dangers of the big city. Likewise, when the Sanhedrin voted on Jesus' guilt, Joseph's was the only dissenting vote, the mark of a conscientious man who would rather struggle with the deeper questions of the case than opt for the convenience of a hasty and dishonorable verdict. And his decision to bury Jesus suggests a human being with questions about who this criminal was.

> "Hunting God is a great adventure."
> —Marie De Flors

As a man with both a healthy curiosity and the official responsibility, as a member of the government, to stay abreast of the political and religious intrigues of the time, Joseph would no doubt have paid close attention to Jesus and his ministry. He would have heard Jesus expound upon the Scriptures, learned of the miracles he performed and the people he touched, and known of his gentle demeanor, his moral rectitude, and his commitment to a life of material simplicity and nonviolence. But he also would have heard Jesus tell the crowds that *he alone* was sent to fulfill the law and the prophets (Matt. 5:17); that he did "not come to bring peace, but a sword" (Matt. 10:34); and that, regarding wealth, "it is easier for a camel to go through the eye of a needle than for a rich man to enter the kingdom of God" (Matt. 19:24). Joseph would surely also have known of the frequent verbal jousting matches Jesus got into with Pharisees and other religious leaders over the correct way to interpret laws and customs. Like a child of the city beholding her first great campfire, Joseph was both intrigued and a little taken aback by the strength of conviction that came forth from this man of courage and controversy.

So the roots of Joseph's decision to ask to bury Jesus in his own tomb may have gone deeper than a desire to honor a Hebrew law or even to perform a charitable act. He may have had a sense of the unfinished, may have been bound to his search for the kingdom and his curiosity as to whether there was something so special about this man that even in his death he had something to tell Joseph about the elusive object of his search. But while it's quite possible that Joseph, like others, received the news two days later that the tomb was empty, there is no reason to believe that this news alone answered his questions. We lose sight of him too quickly; we hear nothing of his journey beyond his one beautiful gesture. His fate, for us, is elusive as well, and forever will be.

## Love Your Enemy

But there may have been one other piece to the puzzle, another explanation as to why Joseph chose to take the fallen Christ and lay him in the tomb: perhaps, like others, as he came to know Jesus, Joseph also came to see something of himself in Jesus. Both men were pilgrims of a sort, who found their calling far from the security of their quiet homelands. Both assumed contrarian positions in the face of popular opinion, and both saw fit to do the kindnesses that others overlooked. As a result, he probably enjoyed the respect of some and endured the scorn of others. They were men of influence and wisdom, and no doubt dispensed each quality with great care and forethought. They were pious men who did not wear their piety on their sleeves but practiced it in modest ways often known but to God.

And perhaps above all else Joseph, "a seeker of the kingdom," saw in Jesus a similar spiritual restlessness, an impatience with an ethically listless people, the desire to recapture the passion that grounded their faith and with that faith an intimation of the kingdom, if not come, then at least coming. Jesus, who recognized that people were sharp on the letter of the law but dull to its spirit, was so eager for them to grasp its power that he took the law to its radical extreme. "You have heard that it was said, 'You shall love your neighbor and hate your enemy,'" Jesus told his followers as he cited Levitical law. "But I say to you, Love your enemies, and pray for those who persecute you" (Matt. 5:43–44). And, as always, he plumbed the depths of the law until he found its very essence. It was in that essence that people would come to understand the law as a living response that emanates from the heart. The law was too precious, too rich to be mere intellectual calisthenics that stay lodged in the head.

Joseph's decision to accept responsibility for Jesus' body was a grand and loving gesture that followed the law, but perhaps a necessary one as well, because no one else seems to have stepped forward to do it. When none of his followers was there to walk the last mile with their fallen savior, as their laws dictated they should, Joseph came and walked two with the body of a man he may never have even met.

When last we hear of Joseph, he seems to me to be at a point in his journey where he may have thought that he had learned what he could from Jesus, this man who was in so many ways like himself. Joseph might not have come to know precisely what he was looking for as he searched out the kingdom—a new nation? interior peace? justice for the oppressed?—let alone found it. But he would find great comfort in tirelessly seeking it, because there is integrity in the pursuit of such a thing. In seeing Jesus as he did, he saw perhaps a partial and idealized reflection of himself and understood that a good life is lived as though what we seek is close at hand and well worth the effort. And that reflection was what gave Joseph the inspiration to leave home for parts unknown and the stamina to become a man of learning. It was what impelled him to live a life of charity and quiet valor, providing both the motivation and the courage to make his request of Pilate. And it is what supplied him with what William Sloane Coffin calls a holy impatience with hairsplitting legalisms, when what is really called for is radical faith—the difference between meticulously measuring the distance of a mile and gladly walking a second one.

Mystery is inseparable from faith, however, and all the secrets of the kingdom were not made known to Joseph, any more than they are made known to us today. Even Jesus, in those last hours and days, was seeking and pursuing, and as he did so, he knew one thing and believed another: He knew he was soon to die, and he believed that only when he did so would the river straighten to meet him.

## A Movement toward the Good

So if Joseph saw a little of himself in Jesus, can we see a little of ourselves in Joseph? What does our pursuit look like? The theologian Paul Tillich once described God as "our ultimate concern," by which he meant that our God is whatever is primary in our life, whatever means more than anything else. So Tillich would have us ask ourselves, what is it that concerns us *ultimately*? What is it that, like Diogenes' one honest man or Quixote's impossible dream, we pursue with such singleness of purpose as to eclipse all other matters of earthly relevance?

Our answers are as varied as our fingerprints, which is perhaps why there are so many different images of the kingdom in Scripture and lore. But I suspect that if we take seriously the example set by this one Arimathean, our answer will be to live decently in the face of the ambiguities with which life is visited—to do good deeds that don't get rewarded, take risks in the name of honor, and choose substance over image, principle over expediency, and hard truths over easy illusions.

I am heartened when I think of the many biblical images of restless seeking, of movement in search of a kingdom, however obliquely defined. I think, for instance, of the exodus itself, for what was that flight out of Egypt if not the abandonment of sure hardship in the name of the very unsure promise that a better life lay somewhere else? And centuries later, after empires had risen and fallen, the return from exile marked the journey taken by people who for two generations had been cut off from the homeland of their faith. Later still, there were the shepherds and the wise men who traveled far to find the child who they believed embodied, in the words of the great hymn, "the hopes and fears of all the years." And finally, when on that first Easter morning the women came to anoint the body but found instead an empty tomb, what did the mysterious young man tell them but, "*Go*, tell his disciples and Peter that he is going before you to Galilee; there you will see him" (Mark 16:7). The first message from the risen Christ to his followers was to be on their way, to be restless, to seek, to follow, and perhaps even to find.

And to the journeys of our biblical forebears we can add our own journeys: Yankee pilgrims and their courageous departure from the shores of England in the name of religious freedom; the Underground Railroad and the brave women and men who risked their lives in the interest of justice; the great marches for women's rights, civil rights, workers' rights, and the right of all children to grow up in a world free of nuclear weapons. These and other searches have been suffused with the energy of the restless and sustained by the stamina of the diligent. And so many of the participants have drawn deeply upon their faith for wisdom and courage, that they might be enlightened by their beliefs and inspired in their actions.

But let's also remember that when Joseph acted, he did so alone. As seekers we aren't constrained to act out that blessed restlessness in the company of others or simply for public consumption. When I think of quiet gestures of unsolicited kindness, I think of Jack McConnell. Jack was for many years a successful physician in suburban Maryland; when he and his wife retired to a comfortable home on an island off the coast of South Carolina, he fully expected to live out his days in irenic bliss.

It didn't take long for Jack's retirement to be disrupted by his realization that his new neighborhood was a two-class island: the very rich and the very poor. He could not abide this with a clear conscience; so in short order Jack began to bring volunteer medical services and donated medical supplies to the folks on the island who needed it. But what really interested me about his story was not the considerable success he's enjoyed doing this but the motivation that got him to do it in the first place.

It was simple, really. Every evening of his youth, when the family would gather for their evening meal—he, his six brothers and sisters, his mother, and his Methodist minister father—they would go around the room and all nine of them would answer one single question the dad would pose. It was the same question, day in and day out: "And what did you do for someone today?"[3]

There are three things I love about this family ritual. First, it is the equivalent of Joseph's search for the kingdom, insofar as it speaks to the idea of restlessness. It invites us to think of bettering the world—or at least that portion of it in our care—the way Coleridge thought of Xanadu: as a forever unfinished project that we can gladly labor over day in and day out. Our eye is not on the destination but on the road itself.

Second, by making the question a part of our daily life we make it a constant companion, which means that we go through our days thinking not only of our own desires but of others' needs. A poet once wrote of how a particular experience must be taken in, learned, and then, most importantly, *forgotten*, by which he meant it must become so much a part of the fabric of our being that we no longer have to bring it to mind. It rides with us.

Finally, I love the fact that it is both concrete and manageable. None of us is able to conquer the world's evils, but all of us are able to resist being conquered by them. I can't cure the homelessness that afflicts my city, but I can donate a little time to a local sweat-equity renovation project. I can't cure AIDS, but I can stop by the hospital for an hour or so and hold the love-starved AIDS babies, whose fates have been

> "We must not, in trying to think about how we can make a big difference, ignore the small daily differences we can make, which over time add up to big differences that we often cannot foresee."
> —Marian Wright Edelman

so unfair and whose futures are so uncertain. And I can't make Eden of a fallen world, but I can buy groceries for my elderly neighbor, pay a compliment to a stranger, pick up litter I find on the street, or write a letter to a senator or a check to a charity.

Like the the kingdom Joseph never found, there is something truly enriching about the quest itself, for as the angel said to the woman that morning, "The one you seek is not here." And so they went, and they looked for him.

# What Cleopas Didn't Know

*There is a wisdom of the head, and a wisdom of the heart.*
—Charles Dickens[1]

*That very day two of them were going to a village named Emmaus, about seven miles from Jerusalem, and talking with each other about all these things that had happened. While they were talking and discussing together, Jesus himself drew near and went with them. But their eyes were kept from recognizing him. And he said to them, "What is this conversation which you are holding with each other as you walk?" And they stood still, looking sad. Then one of them, named Cleopas, answered him, "Are you the only visitor to Jerusalem who does not know the things that have happened there in these days?"*
—Luke 24:13–18

*I*t's been almost two thousand years since Cleopas and his unnamed friend started that conversation on the road to Emmaus about all the "things that had happened," and we still haven't finished it today. To some of us—and to some of Cleopas's contemporaries—Jesus' death ushered in a new era; others believed it was the apocalypse, the beginning of the end of time. Some see it as a crowning triumph, others as a crushing defeat, some as fact, some as metaphor, and some as myth. Others see it as a kind of celestial poetry where truth is in the eyes of the beholder; it is what you think it is. And others still just aren't sure what to make of it: Did he really die? Did he rise from the dead? If so, what conclusions are we to draw? And is it over, or is there to be a second coming?

This last question gives me the patience to tolerate Cleopas's failure to recognize the stranger in their midst. He can't figure out the ending of a whodunit I've already read. To me it's all so clear in retrospect; so why doesn't he see the clues and anticipate where this story is headed? Why doesn't he get it? After all, Jesus *said* he was coming back, didn't he? When he was going from Samaria to Jerusalem, didn't he tell them then, "[I] will be delivered to the Gentiles, and will be mocked and shamefully treated and spit upon; they will scourge [me] and kill [me], and on the third day [I] will rise" (Luke 18:32–33).

But then he also said he would return *again*, or so it seems (this is another one of those questions we're still asking), and if it were to happen in my lifetime, in my town, in my presence, I'm not entirely sure *I'd* know him either. My eyes would be kept from recognizing him. It's a chapter in the whodunit I haven't yet read, one that hasn't yet been written. And its ending is anyone's guess, for most people today who claim to be the savior of the world are more likely to be greeted with medication than adulation.

## Tentative Steps on the Road to Emmaus

We'll never know what Cleopas was thinking that day, but it was a turbulent time for him, and this turbulence would have colored those thoughts. I have to believe his mind was in many places, none of them good. He must've been a close follower of Jesus, because he was with the disciples when Mary and Joanna came and told them of the empty tomb. So not only was he grieving, but he knew that if his loyalty to Jesus were public knowledge, his life, like those of the disciples, was in peril. And if he was married, and if he had children, how could he not think of what peril he put *them* in because of his beliefs?

Perhaps too he had thought Jesus was immortal and held, until Jesus' last breath, that he would come down from that cross as final proof of his divine nature and save all those who risked their lives

My friend David Taylor tells the story of a country minister who has gone into the city to have some dental work done. He is still a little woozy from the anesthetic but begins the drive home. On the way, he stops by a liquor store and picks up the month's supply of communion wine. He is driving back to the church, when suddenly a deer jumps in front of his car. He slams on the brakes, momentarily loses control of his car, and drives up on the sidewalk. In the process the wine bottles crash into each other and shatter, and the wine spills over both the front seat and the minister himself. When the police arrive, they find a man who slurs his words, can't walk a straight line, has run his car up onto a curb, and reeks of alcohol.

"What's your story?" the cop asks, and it dawns on the dejected clergyman how preposterous it all will sound.

"Can you imagine," David asked me, "telling the cop, 'Well, the wooziness and slurred speech are from a dentist's appointment in a town far from here, the car is up on a curb because of a deer you will never find, and the smell is of communion wine that has gone everywhere but down my throat! And I expect you to believe this.'"

Then David added, "And yet, we stand up in the pulpit on Sunday mornings, and we tell our congregation, 'He was the Son of God, but he died. But then he came back to life two days later. He promised salvation, but there is still sin. Oh, and by the way, he says he is coming back one day.' And we expect them to believe *this*."

to follow him. When this didn't happen, how could he not feel dejected, demoralized, and even betrayed by this man who had promised them salvation and paradise and left them with only danger and doubt? And what should Cleopas do now? The instructions Jesus left were a little vague, couched as they were in parables about vineyards, lost sheep, and prodigal sons. Cleopas ran the very real risk of being arrested by any Roman soldier who had little patience with the Nazarene rebel and his motley acolytes. I don't know how persuasive he would have sounded before a hostile judge, answering accusations of sedition with, "Well, your honor, it's this way; a sower went out to sow his seeds . . ."

In any case, preoccupied with their thoughts, with their fates and with their feelings, Cleopas and his companion made their way to Emmaus. They were deep in conversation, but they were distracted by a stranger who asked them what they were talking about.

Cleopas answered the man in a way that revealed much of what was in his heart.

Overwhelmed by what had occurred, he asked, "Are you the only visitor to Jerusalem who does not know the things that have happened?" It's clear that Cleopas revered the man who was crucified, for he referred to him as "Jesus of Nazareth, who was a prophet mighty in deed and word." And what's just as clear is that he was in a state of emotional conflict; he was stranded between deep discouragement and a sense of hope. While he said, "But we had hoped that he was the one to redeem Israel," he also told the stranger that the women "came back saying that they had even seen a vision of angels, who said that he was alive" (Luke 24:21, 23). In the end Cleopas was anything but certain that good will prevail: "Some of those who were with us went to the tomb, and found it just as the women had said; but him they did not see" (Luke 24:24). With this comment, Cleopas really spoke for all of us; we are all awed, we are all reverent, we are all at times discouraged and at times hopeful, and, above all, we are all uncertain, as we have been for two millennia, because to live in faith is to live with questions.

## The History of Salvation

Jesus was eager to answer the questions of Cleopas and his companion because he wanted them to know that there was reason to hope and that their history as Jews could be a source of that hope. But before he could answer, he had to create a new context for them, a context that would help them understand that miraculous things happen even in the face of dire circumstances. He began by asking them, rhetorically, "Was it not necessary that the Christ should suffer these things and enter into his glory?" In other words, he was saying, consider everything you have learned, but do so in light of the promise of the glory, the triumph, the salvation that arises from the gloom of death. After saying this, "beginning with Moses and all the prophets, he interpreted to them in all the scriptures the things concerning himself" (Luke 24:26–27).

Consider, he would have taught them, the history of Israel, how God promised to lead the Hebrews to the land of milk and honey, and how every time they encountered crisis, he delivered them. When the Hebrew community was not even the most fleeting thought to Abraham and Sarah, the future of Israel came forth from the womb of a woman who by every measure was a lifetime past her childbearing years. When their ancestors were in chains, slaves to Pharaoh, they launched an exodus against a mighty empire. When they hungered, manna fell from heaven, and when they were imperiled, seas parted to swallow their enemies. Years later, even in defeat and disgrace, a remnant community emerged to restore their heritage, rebuild their temple, and reclaim their faith. Again and again, as Jesus taught them, the song of the psalmist reverberated throughout history: "I hear a voice I had not known: 'I relieved your shoulder of the burden; your hands were freed from the basket. In distress you called, and I delivered you'" (Psalm 81:5–7). Just as a child struggles from the darkness of the womb to the glory of life, so too would the faithful struggle through the darkness of their doubts, only to emerge to a glory that affirms God's abiding presence in their lives.

By this, Jesus was telling them to hear their history as salvation history, that is, to think of God not as removed from the flow of time but as part of it. He was reminding them that the world is a perilous place, that perils beset us, sometimes of our own making, and that suffering is therefore a part of life. None of that changed on Good Friday or on Easter Sunday. But he was also telling them that the suffering which leads to glory—the suffering that God shares with them and will ultimately deliver them from—is embedded in their past and embodied in their Christ.

What Jesus told them was not enough to make them see it was him, but it was enough to entice them to want to hear more; so when they reached their destination, "they constrained him, saying, 'Stay with us, for it is toward evening and the day is now far spent.' So he went in to stay with them" (Luke 24:29). They wanted more, but it was not by knowledge alone that his message was carried to them. Instead, when they settled in for a meal, the unexpected happened. "When he was at table with them, he took the bread and blessed, and broke it, and gave it to them. And their eyes were opened and they recognized him; and he vanished out of their sight" (Luke 24:30–31). He fed them, but this time he fed them not knowledge, but mystery. He showed them that while they had to learn from the past, to truly know him in their hearts was to find him in the immediacy of the moment. He broke bread with them, recalling fresh memories of the last supper he had shared just days earlier, on the night of his arrest, and their eyes were opened, and they saw him. In this most simple and yet intimate of gestures he was revealed.

In teaching them, and then in ritually reenacting his sacrifice, he did what he did throughout his ministry: he reminded them to learn and to love; to be diligent to the way that God has worked in history, but also to be companions to one another (indeed, the word *companion* literally means, "one who has bread with"). Jesus gave an invitation to share of our harvest, to sit at meals, say a blessing, and remember what great mystery the bread has come to symbolize for those who choose to follow him.

He revealed himself in this way, and then he was gone, vanished. He was no longer needed there; anything else he said would have been superfluous. Now and in the future it would be up to them to learn, to be open to God's word, and to remember him in the breaking of the bread. It would be up to them to be seekers, to ask the questions we're still asking.

The reaction of Cleopas and his friend is important, I think, for they now understood that when they were on the road with Jesus and he was instructing them, something was different. Though his stories were old ones that they had heard many times before, they were hearing them for the first time in light of God's love being made manifest to them through Jesus' life and death. The stories stirred them in ways they had never known before. "Did not our hearts burn within us while he talked to us on the road, while he opened to us the scriptures?" (Luke 24:32) they asked of one another, allowing that a strange feeling entered them as they listened to him, one they may not have trusted at first and could not explain until the moment when he was made known to them.

All of this is to say that they needed *both* the wisdom of the stories and the symbolism of the shared meal, as do we. The stories, Scripture, history need to be told and retold, bequeathed, as the prophet Ezekiel put it, to our children and our children's children. For by these links with the past and with those who have preceded us, our sense of community is preserved and with it our sense of a God not removed from the world but historically at work in it. And then in our rituals—in breaking bread, in the silence of meditation, in the singing of our hymns, in gatherings around home hearths and prayer circles, in town meetings and polling places and family reunions—we confirm that sense of community, of communion, of being bound to one another, and of God not only at work in history but *with us.*

They would not have known him in the breaking of the bread, had he not first taught them to see their history as a history of salvation. And likewise, they could not know him in the telling of the tales, had he not then ritually given himself to them in that modest loaf—manna from heaven, the bread of life, daily bread, broken for them. In bread and word together a community is born that now must find its way without him, for he is gone. As an old Spanish proverb has it, "With bread and wine you can walk down your road" (Con pan y vino se anda el camino).

## The Road That Noes Not End

In many ways we are still on that road, in that moment, alternately uncertain and knowing. Like Cleopas and his friend, we may begin our journey scared and discouraged, because circumstances in our lives or in our world have left us feeling far from God. I think of the more glamorous citizens in my own city, New York, whose homes conjure up the grandeur of Versailles or the baroque excesses of the Gilded Age. And I know others whose home is the church basement, with its linoleum floors and its fluorescent lights, its institutional smell, secondhand linens, meals served up by Scout troops, students, or Sunday school classes. Many of the rich are idle, while many of the poor are not. And we wonder where justice is to be found. We feel similar discouragement in other ways, as well, ways very public and ways very intimate: an old friend refuses to forgive us an old slight, and we don't understand why. A doctor calls and wants to speak with us about a shadow she's spotted on the X-ray. A cross is burned on a front lawn or a swastika painted on a tombstone. A dis-

> "It was a slow day
> and the sun was beating
> on the soldiers by the side of the road.
> There was a bright light,
> a shattering of shop windows.
> The bomb in the baby carriage
> was wired to the radio"
> —Paul Simon[2]

cotheque is blown up in Tel Aviv, or a family planning clinic in Alabama. And we are left on the brink of Oscar Wilde's lament that "something was dead in all of us, and what was dead was hope."[3]

But just when those circumstances threaten to force us off course altogether, just before the whisper of hope is drowned out by the din of indifference, a stranger, or a strange thing, comes into our lives and we are reborn. A parishioner, Sandra, once told me about her younger brother Burt. Always a bright boy but never a happy one, Burt became involved as a young man in a string of bad business deals and worse marriages. A friend acquainted him with cocaine as a palliative for his pain, and, as his sister sardonically put it, "it was the one thing he had a real talent for." From there came the arrests, the rehabs, the relapses, the promises, the broken promises, until one day he disappeared. Weeks went by with no news. The weeks became months, and then years. They had despaired of ever hearing from him again when one Thanksgiving morning he stood at Sandra's front door. The family was delirious with joy—and relief.

"My brother knew we always celebrated Thanksgiving at my home," she told me. "So he knew where to find us. It turns out that when he disappeared things got worse, but then he slowly began pulling his life together. But he didn't want to come back, didn't want, as he put it, 'to present himself to us,' until he felt sure he could get on top of his problems and stay there. That Thanksgiving morning Burt had been clean and sober for just over four years. He had a job—a modest one, but a steady one—and he had a purpose. He wanted simply to live—and to return to the family again.

My mother told him, 'Son, you never left.' " That night they broke their bread and had their feast. And their eyes were opened, because they saw the glory of a man reborn.

It's not an easy road to travel, the one to Emmaus. Hopes dissolve into heartaches, and dreams become disappointments. But traveling this road is worth the trouble and worth the risk. It is the road that takes a person back to his home and his family; and in this way it is the road of the prodigal. It is the road that takes common citizens to the great capitals of the world, the road marched on by Las Madres de los Desaparecedos (The Mothers of the Disappeared) in Buenos Aires, the pacifists in Washington, D.C., and the *Solidarnosc* unionists in Warsaw; and in this way it is the road to freedom.

But it is also the road down which these common citizens—you and I—talk with one another, as did Cleopas and his friend, about those things that lift our hearts and that weigh heavy on our souls. We talk to one another about the nature of faith and in so doing deepen our own. We talk about where salvation comes from and in so doing recognize portals to it we never had considered before. And of course what we are really talking about is how we might better love our God, ourselves, our world, our friends, and above all, our enemies. We will carry on the conversation begun so many years before, the eternal flame of wondering and hoping, teaching and learning, being companions to one another. And in a moment's recognition, it will dawn on us that we are not alone. We will have been joined by a stranger. But no, it is no stranger. It is God, in whatever guise, being made known to us.

# Doubting Thomas

*Life's uncertain voyage.*

—William Shakespeare[1]

*Now Thomas, one of the twelve, called the Twin, was not with them when Jesus came. So the other disciples told him, "We have seen the Lord." But he said to them, "Unless I see in his hands the print of the nails, and place my finger in the mark of the nails, and place my hand in his side, I will not believe."*

—John 20:24–25

## Into the Darkness

In 1655 the poet John Milton wondered, in his poem "On His Blindness," how he could still serve his God as best he knew how and at the same time come to terms with his affliction. Milton, forty-three years old, after losing his sight steadily for about ten years, had been totally blind for about three years when he wrote:

> When I consider how my life is spent
> ere half my days, in this dark world and wide,
> and that one talent which is death to hide,
> lodged with me useless, though my soul more bent
> to serve therewith my Maker . . .[2]

The poem wasn't a big hit with the church. This kind of questioning was just not done in seventeenth-century England.[3] It was a contentious time in England. King Charles had been deposed and executed, Lord Cromwell was in command, the fight for the soul of the church was pitched, and the faithful were expected to hew a conservative course through troubled waters. Against this backdrop the church interpreted the poem as questioning the inscrutable ways of the Almighty and believed Milton's faith in a loving God was on the wane. Some critics called the poem apostasy, an affront to God and to all faithful people.

Like many of us, and no doubt like the disciple Thomas, Milton was profoundly influenced by his life experiences; that is, his beliefs were always subject to reconsideration, refinement, and reinterpretation. So were his doubts. So, while prior to his affliction his experiences led him to hold an orthodox line toward God's ways, his blindness (the creeping darkness that enveloped him) forced him to think again about the wisdom of that orthodoxy. No longer merely submissive to the conventions of the church, Milton now wondered aloud why God would allow his sight to desert *him* of all people, a man whose gift it was to uncover the splendor in what he saw and present it to others in the sublime and enduring lilt of verse and phrase.[4]

For Thomas the seed of doubt was the loss of not his sight but his savior. Thomas's life experience had been one of sitting at the knee of an extraordinary man whose deeds were great and whose message was greater, and Thomas, according to Scripture a man of simple mind but fierce devotion, was in his thrall. Thomas drew deeply from the well of Jesus' wisdom, delighted in his gifts of preaching and prophecy, and marveled at his courage to challenge the assumptions of the status quo. But then, as the hour of death came to Jesus—the curtain of the temple tearing, the earth trembling, and rocks splitting in two—every hope that had accrued in the mind of this disciple, perhaps the most eager to believe of all of them, crumbled under the weight of doubt. The bright promise that Jesus so often made to them—that love would conquer death—now dimmed, like the "dark world and wide" in which Milton lived, to at best a faint hint and at worst a cruel hoax.

## On the Marriage of Doubt and Faith

I am grateful for the story of Thomas, because it provides a room for doubt in the house of faith. I confess that I easily tire of fundamentalists who, like Milton's church, believe that the only true faith is the one that brooks no questions about the ways of God. I am impatient with those who try to explain away inexplicable human suffering by associating it with divine intent to such an extent that when a young child is killed by a drunk driver or a famine blankets parts of Africa, the only response they can muster runs along the lines of, "It is beyond our comprehension, but it must be God's will." And I do not suffer gladly those whose faith is predicated on a need to treat the Bible as though it is a historical regurgitation of ancient days. Such a reading cheapens the writings, robs them of their beauty, and, most important, robs us of our responsibility to think in a discerning way about how these ancient stories were constructed and what they mean to us today.

> "The wise of heart is called a man of discernment."
> —Proverbs 16:21

Life's questions are too complex to be answered—greeting-card style—with simplistic quotes that ignore their theological or literary context. Physical science has challenged our assumptions about the creation of the earth and social science about the supremacy of one religion above all others. And history, the steely-eyed chronicler of human beings at their best and worst, has certainly disabused us of the notion that goodness is uniformly rewarded and evil uniformly punished.

So I am glad that Thomas had his doubts. We are entitled to ours as well. In 1995 in Oklahoma City, some months after Timothy McVeigh leveled the Alfred Murrah office building with a homemade bomb and took the lives of 169 people, I had a discussion with a local psychotherapist by the name of Ronald Mahn. A serious, thoughtful, and spiritual man, Mahn had been working with the surviving families, particularly the parents of the young children who were in the building's first-floor day-care center. A great many of them had their doubts too.

One of Mahn's more poignant observations about his time with these folks had to do with the religious underpinnings of their lives. "This is by and large a pretty religiously conservative town," he pointed out to me. "A great many folks have been raised and nurtured on the idea that if they lead good and faithful lives then God will reward them commensurately.

"When their husband or wife or child died in that horrific blast, many of them threw themselves into their faith, not only for comfort, but to understand, as one woman who lost her daughter put it to me, 'why God did this to me.' But the old formula didn't fit. The assurances they had been given to believe in—in fact, to stake their faith on—were no longer sufficient to explain either the magnitude of their pain or the arbitrariness of its source."

And he later remarked, "These are people who, if they remain people of faith, will come to believe in a very different God than the one they believed in up until that terrible day. The doubts and misgivings that were raised by this one experience will see to that."[5]

## To Live the Questions

Doubt is not only compatible with religion; it is congruent with it. When we ask the questions that arise from our doubts, we are engaging in a profoundly religious exercise. In the Talmud, for example, a holy book of Judaic laws, two learned rabbis debate the meaning of the Torah, the Law. As Jacob Neusner, a Judaic studies scholar, explains it, "In the Talmud you're reading the story of two very holy men questioning what God meant by the laws He bestowed on the Hebrews and how they are going to be interpreted for later generations. It is a debate God expects us all to engage in.

"In fact, many of us believe that when God 'made man in His image'—what Christians call the imago Dei—what he was talking about was giving us the gift of rational thought. Our ability to think, to reason, and to question, parallels God's brooding over creation. No other animal has this capacity, so when we are using it we are acting in God's image."[6]

As the poet Rainer Maria Rilke advised a young protégé who was desperate for absolutes, for ironclad answers to life's thorniest questions,

> Love the questions themselves, as if they are locked rooms or books written in a very foreign language. . . . Live the questions now. Perhaps then, some day in the future, you will gradually, without even noticing it, live your way into the answer.[7]

This process of "living the questions" is a part of our growth. And growth is often painful, whereas absolutes can be of great comfort to us. We want the doctor to assure us that the surgery will go well. We want to know that our job is secure and that the raise is in order. We want to be promised that the child will be born healthy and grow up safe. We want guarantees that our marriage proposal will be accepted, that our dad will make it to his ninetieth birthday, that the accident we heard about on the radio didn't involve anyone we know. We want to know there is a heaven, with a place for us and our loved ones.

But there are no guarantees, and we are left with the fertility of our thought and the courage of our convictions to ask, to wonder how things are as they are, how we can make them better, how our relationship with God can be brought to bear on the great questions of our lives. And, by extension we wonder, what are our old assumptions that don't hold up in the face of new realities?

> "The man who views the world at fifty the same as he did at twenty has wasted thirty years of his life."
> —Muhammad Ali

The grand sweep of our religious tradition holds ample support for what Neusner called "the religiosity of doubt." Sarah laughed at God when God promised her, in her old age, that she would become pregnant and give birth to Abraham's successor. Moses tried to convince God he was not the one to lead the people out of Israel. Job cried out in protest to know why he—a good and righteous man—was visited by calamity. And in Psalm 22 David cried out the lament that Jesus echoed from the cross: "My God, my God, why hast thou forsaken me?"

Like Thomas, these people did not abandon their faith; they simply questioned its assumptions. So Sarah did give birth to the son she named Isaac, which in Hebrew means "laughter." Moses did lead his exodus. Job did have his audience with God. And David, in the Twenty-third Psalm, prayed with complete confidence, "The LORD is my shepherd."

As we grow as thinking, doubting, faithful people, old truisms yield to new, more mature, if also more nuanced and difficult, understandings. Primitive certitudes give way to ambiguity, which in turn gives birth to wisdom. So too with institutions. As members of a church we are identified with an institution that once ordained slavery and refused to ordain women but has reversed course on both issues and is the richer for it. It weans itself from the naive assumptions of creationism and thereby comes to a deeper understanding of the power that symbols wield in the biblical story of our fall from grace. It confesses the sins of the Inquisition and opens its doors—more hesitantly than it should—to fellowship with the religion out of whose loins it first came. And it does all this because it has been willing to ask hard questions about the place of the church in the world and the place of God in the church.

And if we, either as individuals or as institutions, are to continue down this evolutionary path, it will be in large part because we are still willing to ask the kinds of questions that the authors of our venerated texts and documents never had to ask. The Bible tells us nothing directly about stem-cell research or nuclear weapons, about the disenfranchisement of gays, the perils of global warming, or the great questions of life and death that surround euthanasia, abortion, and capital punishment. In these and other instances we will do well to resist facile answers and instead probe the sublime secrets of our Scriptures. We will speak among ourselves the way the Talmudic rabbis did, with wisdom and love. And we will listen for the murmurs of a God who does not call to us from burning bushes, thunder at us from celestial clouds, or sear commandments into slabs of stone.

Life can be reflected in the thoughts of others, but not lived through them. There's a wonderful scene in the movie *Good Will Hunting* in a bar, in which Will, a savant street kid and high school dropout from Boston, overhears an insufferable Harvard student who, trying to impress a couple of women, is giving an impromptu lecture about the agrarian economies of the Southern colonies. "You're a first-year grad student," Will interrupts. "You just got finished reading some Marxian historian, Pete Garrison, probably. You'll be convinced of that until next month when you come upon James Lemmon. Then you'll be talking about how the economies of Virginia and Pennsylvania were entrepreneurial and capitalist way back in 1740.

"That's gonna last until next year, when you'll be in here regurgitating Gordon Wood, talking about, y'know, the pre-Revolutionary utopia and the capitalist formula and its affects on military mobilization."

Frozen in the trap of his own ego, the grad student tells Will, lamely, years down the road, "At least I'll have a degree. And you'll be serving my kids french fries on our way to a ski trip."

"Yeah," Will answers, "but at least I won't be unoriginal."

The growth that springs from doubt is not confined to questions of piety and faith; it is there for us in even the most prosaic moments of our lives. I think of my daughter, Kate, coming of age, prying herself away from her belief in Santa Claus and believing instead in the generosity of her parents. Or my high school friend Larry Grabin, a very bright guy who was raised never to question authority, but went off to college, discovered Thoreau, and shortly thereafter picked up his first picket sign. Or Coleen Rowley, an FBI agent who blew the whistle on the organization she loved because it failed to heed her persistent calls for an investigation that might have prevented the September 11 disaster.

To be open to doubt means to be open—as each of these people was in his or her own way—to new understandings, but also to the possibility of shedding old beliefs that once fit, that may have been held quite dear, but have since been outgrown. With doubt comes the pain and sadness that is often associated with growth. As Paul wrote in his letter to the Corinthians, "When I was a child, I spoke like a child, I thought like a child, I reasoned like a child; when I became a man, I gave up childish ways" (1 Cor. 13:11).

## Blessed Are Those Who Do Not See

Thomas is indispensable to us, because despite his misgivings he was still out there looking, still open to the possibility that Jesus would return. Jesus encountered him on the road, not holed up somewhere in his grief and disenchantment. He is our reminder that doubt invites the hard work of seeking, rather than the coward's refuge of cynicism. His story implies a willingness to allow new thoughts to burrow in and disturb us the way the grain of sand disturbs the oyster's sleep until with much labor the pearl is produced.

Thomas is also indispensable because he was one of the last to see the resurrected Jesus walk the earth. Who among us would not welcome the opportunity to "see in his hands the print of the nails . . . and place [our] hand in his side"? Thomas had to see in order to believe. We, however, have no such luxury; therefore, when Jesus said to him, "Have you believed because you have seen me? Blessed are those who have not seen and yet believe" (John 20:29), he was really speaking to us. Like John Milton, we must make do without sight, must find our way in the darkness and not be overcome by it, must question stale prejudices and be daring enough to assume uncomfortable and even unpopular ways of thinking.

"Where there is much desire to learn, there of necessity will be much arguing, much writing, many opinions; for opinion in good people is knowledge in the making."[8] So said John Milton 350 years ago, and to this may we add only that knowledge is *always* in the making. We are never finished, for it is the seed of wisdom and a cornerstone of informed faith. God only comes to us little by little—daily bread, whispers, and hints—and from these hints we must determine the path of faith that is ours to walk.

# Conclusion: Who He Was, Who We Are

*For God so loved the world that he gave his only Son,*
*that whoever believes in him should not perish but have*
*eternal life.*

—John 3:16

*I*t's not more than about ten miles from the cradle in which Jesus was born to the cross on which he died. He was not a man of the world. Unlike Pilate, for instance, he never wandered very far; never went east of the Dead Sea, west of the Mediterranean, north of Tyre and Sidon or south of Judea except for a time of exile in Egypt; in all he covered an area about the size of Connecticut, and did so spottily. Unlike Caesar, during his earthly life he was not known to the vast majority of the world outside the borders of Palestine and, quite possibly, to the majority within those borders either. His ministry lasted only three years; by comparison, that of his contemporary, the great rabbi Yochanan Ben Zakkai, lasted for over forty. It was a modest career in all ways except one: In the eyes of many, he was a window to God. And as danger gathered around him in those final days and hours, the substance of that divinity drew sharply into focus, if only in retrospect. In the end, his mission and his message was all about love, or, more to the point, it was all about divine love distilled into human form.

## We Cannot Speak of God, but We Can Speak of Love

"Anything we say about God we're really saying about ourselves,"[1] observed the theologian Paul Tillich, by which he meant we can speak of God only self-referentially. If, for instance, I say, "God is merciful," I'm really saying that as I experience God's presence in my life, I experience what I call mercy. If I say God is love, or justice, or anger, or kindness, I am similarly experiencing those characteristics. When the divine enters human form, it becomes something of an approximation, like shadows of the flames in Plato's cave or colors as understood by the blind. We cannot see the infinite face to face, cannot in our finitude articulate it, or describe with language what lies beyond all words; so we are left to speak only of our impressions, to describe the shadows, because the flame itself defies description. And this is where *he* comes in, the one of modest ministry.

Jesus was God's invitation to the people of Palestine—and ultimately, to us—to experience a quality of the divine *as if it were human*; giving us the incomprehensible and the inexpressible, but giving it to us in language we can both comprehend and express, the universal language of selfless love. His work in those few short years and on that narrow stretch of land was the work of wisdom, wonder, and compassion; he taught, he healed, and he cared for the people he met, and in this manner he loved them the way a parent loves a child—patiently, protectively, gently, at times sternly, but always unconditionally. This is the way God loves them, he was showing them; this is the texture of God's affections for them as revealed in their holy texts, their sacred history, their worship, but also in their affairs with one another (for God can be experienced as much in an act of kindness on a city street as in a hymn of praise from a parish pew).

## To Love Us Despite Ourselves

But the past was prologue as that ministry telescoped into those final days; it was now time for the depth and breadth of that divine love to be made manifest. As the British poet Anne Ridler wrote, "Not splendour, but the penal flesh, taken for love, that moves us most."[2] All of the love that he had taught and demonstrated throughout that little patch of land now came into play writ large on the grand stage of Jerusalem; he would now live out his message in the fullest measure, the measure sure to "move us most."

He could have saved his own life but chose not to, and he made this choice because there was no greater expression of love in the face of rejection than to die even for those who did the rejecting. In this, God as much as said, "Even when you turn your back on me, I still love you. Even when you unleash your fury and hurl it in my direction, when you pierce my hands, mock my dignity, or lash my back, I still love you. When you worship other gods, the gods of Ba'al or Isis, or money or fame, the gleaming gods of sabers and swords, of militarism or imperialism, of racism or sexism, of social status or small-mindedness, I will still love you.

"I will love the Roman centurion who arrested me, the one who marched me to my death, the one who nailed me to my cross, and the one who hoisted it high atop Calvary, all of whom did so because they were 'just following orders.' I will love them in their slavish obedience to the rule of others, and I will hope that one day before they die, just once, they will experience the extravagant gift of thinking for themselves.

"I will love the blessed disciples who betrayed, denied, doubted, and abandoned me in my hours of need. I will love the cowardly rulers who protected their own lives by sacrificing mine, and I will love the many in distant lands, across oceans and seas, those long dead, and

> "The worst sinner has a future, even as the greatest saint has a past."
> —Sarvepalli Radhakrishnan[3]

those not yet born, who never knew me or never will. And I will love those of mediocre faith, who revere the Scriptures without reading them, who pray only in need and not in thanks, who give a pittance to the poor and declare themselves generous. I will love the reader of this text and the writer, not because they are great in my eyes but because they are forgiven in my heart."

## Death Be Not Proud

God will love us all in this way, because God wants us to know this one thing: that nothing, "neither death, nor life, nor angels, nor principalities, nor things present, nor things to come, nor powers, nor height, nor depth, nor anything else in all creation, will be able to separate us from the love of God" (Rom. 8:38–39).

If the crucifixion assures us that our sin cannot keep us from God, then the resurrection assures us that neither can death. The empty tomb is emblematic of the strength of divine love expressed in human form, and it is the ultimate gesture of salvation, of overcoming our greatest fear, because it saves us from the fear of our own finitude and from the thought that in the end death will have the final word. God is a creator God, who calls us into being, who knows us before we are born and in every moment of our lives. As the psalmist so gracefully put it,

> Thou didst form my inward parts,
>     Thou didst knit me together in my mother's womb.
> . . . . . . . . . . . . . . . . . . . . . . . . . . . . . . . . . . . .
> when I was being made in secret,
>     intricately wrought in the depths of the earth.
> Thy eyes beheld my unformed substance;
>     in thy book were written, every one of them,
> the days that were formed for me,
>     when as yet there was none of them.
> (Psalm 139:13, 15b–16)

And so the one who knew us before we knew ourselves, who beheld our unformed substance and wrote the days that were formed for us, does not suddenly abandon us when our race has run its course. From the womb to the world, and then to heaven itself, from life, to life, to life, we are with God.

> "Ah Christ, that it were possible
> For one short hour to see
> The souls we loved, that they might tell us
> What and where they be."
> —Alfred, Lord Tennyson[4]

And just as the unborn child, intricately wrought in the depths of the earth, knows nothing about the world that is soon to be her home, so too do we know nothing about the world into which we are born on the occasion of our death. But what we *do* know is that the stone was moved, the tomb was empty, death was overcome, and the love of God that is forbearing enough to endure sin is also mighty enough to surmount death.

## They Are All Still Here; They Are All of Us

Forgiveness is what sin makes necessary and grace makes possible. And for those who claim Jesus as the one who embodies that grace, the story of his Passion cannot be told apart from the stories of the sinners and saints who were there to the very end. This, I believe, is what makes it a timeless tale. Because in these lives, these ordinary lives, the Passion is not an event anchored in the past but a living thing as pertinent now as it was that first Palm Sunday, when this humble king came into his court not in a gilded coach but on a beast of burden. And what makes it pertinent is the fact that to this day nothing has changed. Judas still lives among us in tragic misery, unable to accept his acceptability in the eyes of God. Peter still declares his faith today and renounces it tomorrow. The women are still marginalized exemplars of what it means to be unburdened by ego in the service of another. And all the rest, the good and the bad, the brave and the frightened, the weak and the strong, are still with us, in need of a love they may desperately want, or shrink from, or be oblivious to. They are all there because they are all of us.

## To Live into Salvation

I believe the real worth of the Passion story is found not only in seeing God's hand in Christ's destiny but in seeing our own as well. We are not mere spectators to our own salvation but participants in it. With our every thought and gesture, with every action we take or refuse to take—every time we show compassion to one we do not like or indifference to one we do, every time, when confronted with injustice, we stand firm before mighty tyrants or cower before petty ones—we are either imitating unconditional love or underscoring our eternal need for it.

It is not a matter of choice. If we claim to see in Christ the emergence of the divine, then we have no choice but to define our lives as either encouraging that emergence or resisting it. And perhaps this is the final word: in the story of the Passion—with all of its sinners and all of its saints—we are given a new context for understanding the interplay between God and us. For us salvation comes forth not from above or beyond, not from philosophical constructs or theological queries, but from that little swath of ancient Judean soil. For it is here, in that desert sand, that the stories are embedded; the stories of the people who were there those fateful days, the memories of love and deception, of conviction and doubt, of honor and shame. And just as those people had no choice but to play a part in the unfolding of salvation history, neither do we.

# Notes

## INTRODUCTION

1. Dag Hammarskjöld, *Markings* (New York: Knopf, 1964), 123.
2. Donald Creighton, *Toward the Discovery of Canada* (New York: Macmillan, 1972), 145.
3. From a sermon by the Rev. Gregory Sutterlin, 1979.
4. Cited by Merle Miller in *Plain Speaking: An Oral Biography of Harry S. Truman* (New York: Putnam, 1973), 365.

## CHAPTER 1

1. Pilgrim Hymnal (Boston: Pilgrim Press, 1958), #34.
2. Rainer Maria Rilke, *Letters to a Young Poet* (New York: Vintage, 2004), 68.
3. Martin Buber, *I and Thou* (New York: Scribner, 1973), 4.
4. Rudolf Otto, *The Idea of the Holy* (Oxford: Oxford Press, 1958), 3.
5. Harry Emerson Fosdick, *The Meaning of Service* (Nashville: Abingdon Press, 1920), 63.
6. W. H. Auden, *The Dyer's Hand, II, Making, Knowing, and Judging* (London: Faber & Faber, 1975), 2.

## CHAPTER 2

1. Charles Baudelaire, *Les Fleurs du Mal. L'Heautontimoroumenos* (Paris: Magnard, 2002), 133.
2. Osamu Tezuka, *Buddha: Devadatta* (New York: Vertical, 2004), 14.
3. George Bernard Shaw, *The Devil's Disciple* (New York: Heritage Press, 1966), 31.
4. Walt Whitman, "Reconciliation," in *Leaves of Grass* (New York: Signet, 2000), 271.
5. Donald Shriver, personal conversation, 1991.

6. Walt Whitman, "A Sight in Camp at the Daybreak Gray and Grim," in *Leaves of Grass,* 259.

7. Osamu Tezuka, *Buddha,* 14.

## CHAPTER 3

1. Quoted by Lewis Lapham, *Harper's,* April 2004, 17.

2. www.strike-the-root.com.

3. Philo, *On the Life of Moses,* as found in Gunther Plaut, *The Torah Commentary* (New York: Union of American Hebrew Congregations, 1986), 167.

4. Joseph Hertz, *The Torah Commentary* (New York: Union of American Hebrew Congregations, 1986), 194.

5. Walt Whitman, "Passage to India," in *Leaves of Grass* (New York: Signet, 2000), 111.

6. David McCullough, *Truman* (New York: Simon & Schuster, 1992), 353.

## CHAPTER 4

1. James Lowell, "The Present Crisis" (1845), in *The American Tradition in Literature,* vol. 1 (New York: Norton, 1956), 1217.

2. Dorothy Dix, quoted in *Memorable Quotations: American Women Writers of the Past,* Diana Dell, ed. (iUniverse, Lincoln, NE: 2000).

3. André Gide, recalled on his death, in *Simpson's Contemporary Quotations* (Boston: Houghton Mifflin, 1988), 228.

4. Thomas Mann, *Death in Venice* (New York: Vintage, 1989), 82.

5. Joe Mullin, personal conversation, 2003.

6. Anaïs Nin, quoted in *Memorable Quotations: American Women Writers of the Past,* Diana Dell, ed. (iUniverse, Lincoln, NE: 2000).

7. Reinhold Niebuhr, *The Irony of American History* (New York: Scribner, 1952), 242.

## CHAPTER 5

1. Lesley Conger, *Adventures of an Ordinary Mind* (New York: Norton, 1963), 76.

2. Mario Cuomo to Roger Rosenblatt, 92nd Street Y, New York, December 2001.

3. Desmond Tutu, private conversation, 1994.

## CHAPTER 6

1. Quoted in George Plimpton, *Writers at Work* (New York: Viking Press, 1963), 111.

2. Saul Alinsky, *Rules for Radicals* (New York: Vintage, 1989), 74.

3. Aldous Huxley, recalled on his death, *New York Herald Tribune*, November 24, 1963.

4. George Sand, *The Haunted Pool* (Santa Cruz, CA: Shameless Hussy Press, 1978), 54.

## CHAPTER 7

1. Shirley Chisholm, quoted on *Womenshistory.com.*

2. Reinhold Niebuhr, *The Nature and Destiny of Man* (New York: Scribner, 1964), 212.

3. Augustine, *City of God* (New York: Modern Library, 2001), 113.

4. Jerome L., personal conversation with the Rev. Dr. Preston Washington, May 1994.

5. Jeanette Rankin, quoted on *Womenshistory.com.*

## CHAPTER 8

1. William Shakespeare, *Romeo and Juliet* (New York: Oxford University Press, 1999), 414.

2. Irving Bartlett, *Wendell Phillips, Brahmin Radical* (Westport, CT: Greenwood Publishing, 1973), 47.

3. George Appleton, *The Oxford Book of Prayer* (New York: Oxford University Press, 1985), 46.

4. Rainer Maria Rilke, *Letters to a Young Poet* (New York: Vintage, 1971), 84.

## CHAPTER 9

1. Eberhard Bethge, personal conversation, April 1977.

2. Ibid.

3. William Sloane Coffin, personal conversation, 1988.

4. Thornton Wilder, *The Eighth Day* (New York: Harper & Row, 1967), 113.

5. Dom Helder Camara, quoted in William Sloane Coffin, *The Heart Is a Little to the Left* (Hanover, NH: Dartmouth/New England University Press, 1999), 36.

6. Hannah Arendt, *The Life of the Mind* (New York: Harcourt Brace, 1978), 242.

7. Henri Nouwen (public lecture, Yale Divinity School, 1977).

8. Gyorgy Konrad, *The Case Worker* (New York: Harcourt Brace, 1969), 169.

## CHAPTER 11

1. Polybius, *The Rise of the Roman Empire,* trans. Ian Scott-Tilvert (New York: Penguin, 1980), 242.
2. Henry Nouwen (lecture, Yale Divinity School, 1977).
3. The Christian History Institute, Worcester, PA.
4. Elizabeth Rubin, "The Opening of the Wahhabist Mind," *New York Times Magazine,* March 7, 2004, 33.
5. Madeleine L'Engle, "Writer, Wife, Theologian," *Anglican Digest,* Pentecost 1983, 31.

## CHAPTER 12

1. Jean Oddy, *Church Times*, 1988.
2. William Butler Yeats, *A Prayer for My Daughter* (1921).

## CHAPTER 13

1. Rebecca West, *Glimpses of the Great* (Lanham, MD: University Press of America, 1981), 67.
2. Roger Rosenblatt, 92nd Street Y, New York, June 1999.
3. Jack McConnell, "And What Did You Do for Someone Today?" *Newsweek,* June 18, 2001, 13.

## CHAPTER 14

1. Charles Dickens, *Hard Times* (New York: Turtleback, 1977), 8.
2. Paul Simon, "The Boy in the Bubble" on *Graceland,* Warner Brothers, 1997.
3. Oscar Wilde, *The Ballad of Reading Gaol* (New York: Perennial, 1989), 78.

## CHAPTER 15

1. William Shakespeare, *Timon of Athens* (New York: Signet Classics, 1989), 88.
2. John Milton, *The Complete Poems* (New York: Penguin, 1999), 84.
3. Prof. Albert Labriola, Duquesne University, personal conversation, March 2004.
4. Ibid.
5. Ronald Mahn, personal conversation.
6. Prof. Jacob Neusner, Brown University, personal conversation, May 1974.

7. Rainer Maria Rilke, *Letters to a Young Poet* (New York: Norton, 1986), 36.

8. John Milton, "Tractate of Education," in *Complete Prose Works of John Milton* (New Haven, CT: Yale University Press, 1973), 167.

## CONCLUSION

1. Paul Tillich, *Systematic Theology* (Chicago: University of Chicago Press, 1978), 344.

2. Anne Ridler, "Deus Absconditus," in *Collected Poems* (Austin, TX: Harry Ransom Humanities Research Center, 1997), 34.

3. Sarvepalli Radhakrishnan, recalled on his death, *Simpson's Quotations* (New York: Houghton Mifflin, 1988), 238.

4. Alfred, Lord Tennyson, "Maud," in *Tennyson's Poetry*, ed. Robert W. Hill Jr. (New York: Norton, 1999), 309.